Transmedial Narration

Lars Elleström

Transmedial Narration

Narratives and Stories in Different Media

Lars Elleström
Department of Film and Literature
Linnaeus University
Växjö, Sweden

ISBN 978-3-030-01293-9   ISBN 978-3-030-01294-6 (eBook)
https://doi.org/10.1007/978-3-030-01294-6

Library of Congress Control Number: 2018960865

© The Editor(s) (if applicable) and The Author(s) 2019 This book is an open access publication
Open Access This book is licensed under the terms of the Creative Commons Attribution 4.0 International License (http://creativecommons.org/licenses/by/4.0/), which permits use, sharing, adaptation, distribution and reproduction in any medium or format, as long as you give appropriate credit to the original author(s) and the source, provide a link to the Creative Commons licence and indicate if changes were made.
The images or other third party material in this book are included in the book's Creative Commons licence, unless indicated otherwise in a credit line to the material. If material is not included in the book's Creative Commons licence and your intended use is not permitted by statutory regulation or exceeds the permitted use, you will need to obtain permission directly from the copyright holder.
The use of general descriptive names, registered names, trademarks, service marks, etc. in this publication does not imply, even in the absence of a specific statement, that such names are exempt from the relevant protective laws and regulations and therefore free for general use.
The publisher, the authors and the editors are safe to assume that the advice and information in this book are believed to be true and accurate at the date of publication. Neither the publisher nor the authors or the editors give a warranty, express or implied, with respect to the material contained herein or for any errors or omissions that may have been made. The publisher remains neutral with regard to jurisdictional claims in published maps and institutional affiliations.

Cover illustration: Pattern © Melisa Hasan

This Palgrave Pivot imprint is published by the registered company Springer Nature Switzerland AG
The registered company address is: Gewerbestrasse 11, 6330 Cham, Switzerland

Acknowledgments

I would like to thank all of my associates at the Linnaeus University Centre for Intermedial and Multimodal Studies for their support and constantly inspiring ideas and critiques. I am particularly grateful for the help of Liviu Lutas, who went through my manuscript thoroughly and helped me to spot omissions and mistakes. Warm thanks also to my many colleagues around the world who have given me the opportunity to present and discuss my ongoing research at seminars, workshops, and conferences. Finally, I am grateful to Marie-Laure Ryan, who also read the manuscript at a late stage and patiently commented upon its strengths and weaknesses.

CONTENTS

Part I   Drawing the Frame — 1

1   Opening — 3

2   Circumscribing Narration — 21

3   Defining Narration — 35

4   Narrating Through Media Modalities — 45

Part II   Scrutinizing the Essentials — 61

5   Communicating, Narrating, and Focalizing Minds — 63

6   Events — 77

7   Temporal Interrelations — 85

8   Internal Coherence — 95

| 9 External Truthfulness | 103 |

| Part III Demonstrating the Principles | 113 |

| 10 Narration in Qualified Media Types | 115 |

| References | 137 |

| Index | 147 |

PART I

Drawing the Frame

This is a methodical treatise on narration in different media types. It is not focused specifically on what is today thought to be modern media—forms of media that will soon probably be considered rather old-fashioned. Neither is it mainly focused on old media. Rather, it is about media characteristics that are never new and will not ever become old. Similarly, it is not a treatise on old or new forms of narration; it is a theoretical rather than a historical study that should nevertheless be relevant for the understanding of narration in all times, including our own.

The title of this study reveals that it will be about narratives and stories. These notions should not be understood as separate things; later in the study, the story will be defined as the center of the narrative. It is here that one finds those essential transmedial media characteristics that make it possible for dissimilar media types to narrate in the same way, at least partly.

The treatise is divided into three parts. Part I, "Drawing the Frame", presents established concepts and newly developed general concepts that I find indispensable for formulating a nuanced theoretical model of transmedial narration. In Part II, "Scrutinizing the Essentials", I investigate those specific transmedial media characteristics that are most vital for realizing narratives in a plenitude of different media types. Part III, "Demonstrating the Principles", contains some studies in which the narrative potentials of a number of vastly diverse media types are illuminated with the aid of the theoretical framework.

CHAPTER 1

Opening

Abstract This chapter provides a general introduction to the treatise. After a brief background sketch, some basic terminology concerning the field of transmedial narration is covered. This is followed by an overview of existing research in the area and declarations of the central research questions, aims, and goals of the investigation. Finally, an overview of the treatise is presented.

Keywords Transmedial narration • Transmediality • Transmediation • Transmedia storytelling

Everyday communication is full of simple and sometimes also complex narratives that make our lives and our surroundings comprehensible. These narratives are realized in a large variety of media types. On a typical day, I may meet one of my neighbors on my way to the mailbox and she will tell me, using shifting tones and intonations and sometimes vivid gestures, about a weekend trip to her relatives in Gothenburg. At the breakfast table, I read in the newspaper about all sorts of events: accidents and happenings in my region and political developments around the world. The written texts are visually formed in different ways and often combined or integrated with still images that contribute to or tell their own stories. Listening to the radio while brushing my teeth and feeding my cats, I first

© The Author(s) 2019
L. Elleström, *Transmedial Narration*,
https://doi.org/10.1007/978-3-030-01294-6_1

hear a song about a problematic love affair and then an instrumental piece that depicts tensions among several emotional states. When I finally reach my worktable and start my computer, I receive an email from my daughter with a link to a short movie that I decide to watch before starting to work properly. The email tells a short story about the movie, which represents the adventures of a computer mouse.

Therefore, long before I have even had my first cup of coffee I have perceived an abundance of narratives. It is clear that many of these narratives are, or may be, connected to each other. They do not exist in isolation, and there are clearly no definite borders between narratives formed by dissimilar media types. Considering that there are no definitive borders between media types as such—they all overlap each other, in complex patterns of similarities and differences—this is hardly surprising. Media obviously have their communicative capacities because of our cognitive faculties, and it is almost absurd to suggest the notion of a cognitive system working in such a way that representations of events through one kind of medium could not in any way be matched by representations of events through other media forms. A brain that harbors a cognitive system composed of secluded, media-specific strata of information would be dysfunctional.

However, we do have the capacity to communicate about things through different forms of media in such a way that narratives in various media types connect to each other in highly meaningful ways. These connections may be immediate, such as when my neighbor's speech and gestures together narrate about a trip, or when the written texts and still images in the newspaper narrate about a political crisis. However, the connections may also cover temporal gaps: my daughter's email may include a description of the movie that makes it possible for me to anticipate what goes on in it, and it is also possible for me to later tell my wife about what happened in the piece of music that I listened to in the morning.

Basic Terminology

Several complex capacities and phenomena are involved in these communicative occurrences. At the heart of the matter is how narratives may be created beyond specific media types or be moved across media borders; therefore, it is convenient to use terms starting with the Latin prefix 'trans-'—which means 'beyond', 'across', or 'through'—to denote what is going on. As there are several expressions containing 'trans-' and 'media',

I will briefly comment on some central terms here and tie them to succinct conceptual definitions.

From the most wide-ranging perspective, the term 'transmediality' should be understood as referring to the general concept that different media types share many basic traits that can be described in terms of material properties and abilities for activating mental capacities. All media products, in partly similar ways, are physical existences that trigger semiotic activity and can be properly understood only in relation to each other. Thus, physical media properties and semiosis are transmedial phenomena. More specifically, different media types may, to a large extent—although certainly not completely—communicate similar things, such as events forming narratives. Using more technical language, several media types may more or less fully represent "compound media characteristics" of various sorts (Ellestrőm 2014a: 39–45). In other words, represented media characteristics may be transmedial to different degrees. *Transmediality* is evidently a central part of *intermediality*, which is an even broader concept based on the proposition that different media types are interrelated in all kinds of ways.

It is only a short step from the idea that represented media characteristics may be transmedial to different degrees to recognizing that media characteristics, because of their transmedial nature, can be understood as being transferred among different kinds of media. Inserting a temporal perspective, it very often makes sense to acknowledge not only that similar media characteristics are or may be represented by dissimilar media but also that media characteristics that can in some respect be understood as *the same*, recur after having appeared in another medium. The examples of a written email describing the events in a movie and spoken words retelling a musical story both include a temporal gap between what might be called source and target media, but also the implicit notion of sameness. We find the relations between email and movie and between speech and music meaningful because the events that they represent are not only similar but in some respects the same (here, sameness should be understood as a pragmatic rather than a metaphysical quality). I refer to such a transfer of media characteristics as *transmediation*. In our minds, some perceived media characteristics of the target medium are, in important ways, the same as those of the source medium, which is to say that the media characteristics of an initial medium are perceived to be *represented again* by another kind of medium (Ellestrőm 2014a: 20–27).

Building on these brief stipulations, the term 'transmedial narration' should be understood to refer to all varieties of transmediality and transmediation where narration is a media characteristic that is significant enough to be observed. In the most general terms, then, the concept of transmedial narration includes the notion that an abundance of different media types share traits that give them narrative capacities. In more specific terms, transmedial narration also includes the idea that the world is actually full of various sorts of more or less developed and complex narratives communicated by different media types. In its most particular sense, transmedial narration can be understood as transmediation of narratives; the characteristics of narratives can be represented again by dissimilar media types and yet be perceived to be the same despite the transfer.

Transmedial narration, in its most general sense, must be accepted as a reality that has a bearing on a lot of communication. Furthermore, transmediation of narratives is extremely common, not only in everyday communication but also in more complex and official systems of communication such as education, research, and legal processes. It also flourishes in religion, art, and entertainment.

For some years now, Henry Jenkins's concept of *transmedia storytelling* has been popular. This concept refers to the modern phenomenon of building large narratives as a sum of partial narratives distributed by different kinds of media such as motion pictures, comics, video games, novels, and various forms of Internet-based media: "A transmedia story unfolds across multiple media platforms with each new text making a distinctive and valuable contribution to the whole" (Jenkins 2008: 97–98). In fact, this is an old and widespread phenomenon that can be observed in, for instance, Hindu, Greek, and Christian mythologies, although historical and cultural differences can obviously be noted (see for instance Ryan 2013; Mittell 2014). Transmedia storytelling—narratives in different media types working together to form a larger whole—requires that narratives can be largely transmediated. It would not be possible to combine narratives from different media types to a larger whole if these narratives did not overlap. In effect, this means that one recognizes represented media characteristics in the different media as the same; thus, represented persons, environments, ideas, events, and their interrelations can interlock. However, current research in transmedia storytelling does not engage what I consider to be the central questions of transmedial narration: how are such transmediations possible at all and what are their limitations?

Earlier Research

Although views differ considerably regarding most aspects of transmedial narration, the majority of researchers within the area seem to agree that narration is indeed a transmedial concept: media types that are not language-based may also narrate to a certain extent. Narration in various non-verbal media types has been noted, discussed, and to a certain degree theorized for centuries, although it has not been thoroughly conceptualized until recently. Explicit recognition of narration as a transmedial phenomenon can be found from the 1960s onward (Bremond 1964; Barthes 1977 [1966]).

As media characteristics are clearly not either fully transmedial or not transmedial at all, the extent to which and ways in which narration is transmedial has been a principal question since the advent of thorough explorations of the concept. Seymour Chatman, often quoted in the research on transmedial narration, maintained that the "transposability of the story is the strongest reason for arguing that narratives are indeed structures independent of any medium" (Chatman 1978: 20; cf. Altman 2008: 1). Several commentators consider this to be an overstatement; because dissimilar media types have different means for communicating narratives, narrative structures cannot be understood as 'independent' of medium in a strong sense: "Narratives are not so much structures independent of any medium, as structures common to several media" (Walsh 2007: 63). Thus, narratives always depend on some kind of medium to be realized; however, as different media types may generate narratives that are nevertheless recognizable as the same, narrative structures can be understood to be 'independent' of the medium, in a weak sense. Although media differences certainly do make a difference, the "transposability of the story" (Chatman 1978: 20) remains.

To explain the relative dependency on media types, it is imperative to realize that the partly dissimilar and partly shared properties of various media types "both open up possibilities and impose constraints [that] shape the narration" (Rimmon-Kenan 1989: 160)—even though narration is "a process which is not in its basic aims specific to any medium [it] deploys the materials and procedures of each medium for its ends" (Bordwell 1985: 49). Marie-Laure Ryan, who has played an important role in the development of what she calls transmedial narratology, has articulated a nuanced view on the relation between media types and narration: "A core of meaning may travel across media, but its narrative potential will be filled out, actualized differently when it reaches a new medium" (Ryan 2005: 1). Although I share the general views of Rimmon-Kenan, Bordwell, and Ryan on this matter, my way of conceptualizing transmedial narration in this treatise will differ substantially from all of the scholars quoted above (as will be demonstrated in Chaps. 2, 3, and 4).

The questions of how and to what extent narration is transmedial have also been debated in a more implicit way, through a steady flow of articles and books on narration in ever-new media types. Previous investigation in the area of transmedial narration raises some hope that research will be able to map and integrate knowledge about a very large range of different narrative media types. The following list of examples of media that have been investigated from a narratological perspective since the 1970s (especially highlighting early studies of the respective media types) demonstrates impressive breadth. Apart from numerous studies of narration in various forms of written literature, there have been studies on narration in spoken, everyday language (Labov 1972); comics (Hünig 1974; Abbott 1986); painting (Alpers 1976; Steiner 1988: 7–42; Wolf 2003, 2004); literature and film (Chatman 1978); comics and image sequences (Schnackertz 1980); written language, painting, and film (Goodman 1981); history writing (White 1981); painting and reliefs on ancient urns, walls, columns, and sarcophagi (Brilliant 1984); film music (Gorbman 1987); instrumental music (Newcomb 1987; Kramer 1991); drama (Richardson 1988); television news (Campbell and Reeves 1989); written and oral language in the legal system (Brooks and Gewirtz 1998); literature and history writing (Canary and Kozicki 1978; Cohn 1990); mural decoration in churches (Lavin 1990); written language in economics and the natural sciences (Nash 1990); music in general and opera (Abbate 1991; McClatchie 1997); advertisements (Stern 1994); spoken, everyday language and literature (Fludernik 1996); dance (Foster 1996); painting and photography (Kafalenos 1996); maps, diagrams, and advertisements (Kress and van Leeuwen 1996: 45–78); family photographs (Hirsch 1997); hypertext (Hayles 2001); still images and moving images (Ribière and Baetens 2001); film and television programs (Thompson 2003); all kinds of artistic media (Gaudreault and Marion 2004); computer games (Neitzel 2005); radio broadcasts of sports events (Ryan 2006); literature, comics, film, radio play, and hypertext (Mahne 2007); visual diagrams (Ryan 2007); music, literature, and drama (Almén 2008); written and oral language about the self (Eakin 2008); architecture and literature (Psarra 2009); sculpture (Wolf 2011); mathematical proofs (Doxiadis 2012); mathematical diagrams (de Freitas 2012); novels including photographs (Schwanecke 2012); journalism (Berning 2014); music and dance (Kutschke 2015); program music (Liu 2015); musical concept albums and their sleeves (Arvidson 2016); music combined with moving images (Giannoukakis 2016); and board games (Thibault 2016).

This breadth is emphasized even more if one considers the many collections of articles with really wide-ranging scopes of narrative media types. However, as Jan-Noël Thon accurately noted, "a genuinely transmedial narratology is not (or should not be) the same as a collection of media-specific narratological terms and concepts" (Thon 2016: 15). With some exceptions, this succinct observation can be used to criticize the setup of edited collections on narration in visual art, music, poetry, film, and comics (Nünning and Nünning 2002); face-to-face communication, gestures, painting, comics, moving pictures, music, and digital media (Ryan 2004b); literature, comics, television serials, motion pictures, photonovels, photo collections, interactive writing on the Internet, computer games, and advertisements in television and radio (Grishakova and Ryan 2010); computer-mediated communication, video games, political speeches, and film (Hoffmann 2010); television programs, motion pictures, web texts, opera, comics, speech, gesture, and multimodal novels (Page 2010); drama, feature films, graphic novels, video games, literature, visual art, and television series (Ryan and Thon 2014); literature, drama, film, journalism, television news, law courts, and oral communication (Nünning 2015); and film music, songs, rock music, radio drama, video games, audio books, and audio guides (Mildorf and Kinzel 2016b).

Despite this remarkable range, most research on narration is concentrated on verbal media types, with robust narratological traditions in both linguistics and the study of literature. Furthermore, artistic media types, whether they include verbal components or not, dominate the research field. More importantly, one must conclude that the various perspectives on a wealth of media types are anything but broadly integrated. As Thon noted (2015: 441), monographs and articles on transmedial narration, as intermedial research at large—with only a few exceptions (such as Ryan 2006)—consider just one or two media types at a time and are thus transmedial only in a weak sense.

While transmedial narratology is widespread to the extent that there are many studies of narration outside the verbal domain, the field is largely unexplored considering the few studies that seek to discover the common ground of narration in a broad range of media types. Although there has been a lot of research for several decades on transmedial narration, there is presently only a piecemeal understanding of how the fundamentals of a genuinely transmedial theory of narration might look. This is remarkable considering the ubiquity of narratives in various media types in general, and more specifically transmediated narratives in all forms of communication. Notwithstanding several decades of research on the fundamental importance of narratives for humans, a truly transmedial conceptualization of the central features of narration is still lacking. There are still no large-scale studies on transmedial narration in a strong sense, in which truly transmedial concepts useful for analyzing narration in a really broad scope of media types are methodically developed. Considering the diverging conceptualizations in the many studies on narration in various media, I conclude that such a fundamental conceptual framework is much needed.

This is not to say that narration is necessarily a completely transmedial phenomenon. Liviu Lutas's contention that "narration in general can [not] be considered to be a trait that can be found in all media" (Lutas 2016: 33) should be taken seriously. Clearly, not all kinds of media can narrate to the same degree; consequently, there are probably media types whose narrative capacities are so rudimentary that they might just as well be considered non-narrative. For the moment, however, I leave the possible borders of transmediality in narration open so that I can explore the whole media territory without restrictions.

Aims and Goals

It became clear in the previous section that the questions of how and to what extent narration is transmedial have been central in earlier research. They will remain so in this study. I have also already mentioned a couple of related questions that I find imperative: How are transmediations of narratives possible at all, and what are their limitations? The treatise will also be guided by some more specific research questions: How can narration be conceptualized within a broad communicative context, including psychological and cognitive aspects? How can narration be conceptualized so that both its wide-ranging transmedial potential and its media-specific limitations can be accounted for? What are the main constituents of narration understood in a truly transmedial way and how are they related to other central features of communication?

An eloquent quotation from Liv Hausken, expressing views that overlap closely with my own, shows the direction of my aim with this treatise:

> I believe that we should aspire to narrative theories that are independent of medium, while recognizing that the development of such theories demands a certain level of abstraction. Furthermore, I believe that we need medium-specific theories of narrative, theories with a conceptual apparatus sufficiently specialized to define the actual differences between narratives in the various media. In addition to this, we need to be aware of the differences between the two types of narrative theories. The comparative study of narrative in different media, either at the same time or one after the other, is one of the most efficient ways to expose both the common narrative features and the medium-specific aspects of the objects of study. (Hausken 2004: 397)

While I recognize the great value of "medium-specific theories of narrative", my aim is to form a narrative theory that is "independent of medium" and to systematically chart its components to facilitate detection of also "medium-specific aspects". I believe that the most efficient way of doing this is to anchor the conceptualization in a semiotic framework. While much classical narratology has been influenced by linguistic semiotics, especially the work by Ferdinand de Saussure, this is a blind alley for transmedial narratology. Language is only one, albeit very important, means of communication, and in my view all attempts to understand communication at large through essentially linguistic theories are doomed to fail. This is partly why semiotics has gained a bad reputation among some scholars. On the other hand, while the semiotics of Charles Sanders Peirce certainly has its pitfalls, it offers a foundational conceptualization that makes possible a truly transmedial understanding of communicative phenomena. Thus, I will use Peircean semiotics combined with some established theories of cognition and psychology. I will also apply some of my own previously developed concepts on communication, intermediality, and semiosis to structure the treatise.

Naturally, I will also profit from achievements in literary theory where narratology has vital roots. Whereas some of its concepts are very useful also for a transmedial approach, many are media-specific rather than transmedial and are therefore not suitable to deal with in a treatise like this. There is also much terminological and conceptual incongruity in the collected body of narratological research, which leads me to avoid some terms that are used also for denoting potentially transmedial concepts, even though they emanate from language studies. For instance, I will not use the central term 'discourse', which has been employed in many ways that are rather confusingly interrelated. Instead, the central concepts and distinctions that are associated with the term will be described in other ways.

Thus, I will disregard many ideas and concepts that have been discussed for decades in narratology, sometimes because I find them pointless and often because they are overly media-specific, meaning that they may be highly useful within a more limited frame. It is far beyond the purpose of this study to interrogate these many concepts that I choose to exclude. Instead, I will try to create an account of transmedial narration that is clearly focused on what is most distinctively transmedial, largely but not completely avoiding detours that might make my position within the whole narratological field clearer, but would at the same time distract the attention from my commitments.

I am aware of the risks of such an enterprise. In his insightful discussions of the possibility of forming a truly transmedial narratology, Thon noted that the question remains "if decreasing the granularity of just about any narratological concept until it can somehow be applied to a sufficiently large number of narrative media is, in fact, a good idea" (Thon 2016: 23). Although I will certainly not try to adjust "just about any narratological concept" to fit in the transmedial costume, I expect that some readers of this study will find that my aim of forming a radically transmedial concept of narration is not a very good idea. Of course, I believe that it is; transmedial research sometimes demands not only "a certain level of abstraction" (Hausken 2004: 397) but a very high level of abstraction indeed. Although much traditional flesh will have to be carved off the bones (not necessarily to be discarded, but rather to be remolded), I believe that it is only by starting with the naked transmedial skeleton of narration that one can really detect the similarities and differences among more media-specific narratologies.

Therefore, my ambition is to make this treatise more broadly transmedial than the already existing works on transmedial narration, such as Thon's (2016) in many ways exemplary and thorough investigation of some central narratological concepts applied to feature films, graphic novels, and video games. Although Thon's approach is certainly broadly transmedial, it would be quite difficult to include, say, narration in instrumental music or mathematical equations in his framework. A concept such as storyworld, which is central for Thon, presupposes that narratives are understood as representations of concrete, anthropomorphic characters moving around and acting in three-dimensional surroundings. This is not at all a suitable way of conceptualizing narration in media types such as instrumental music—and this is not a far-fetched example, since there is quite extensive research on musical narration from which concepts such as storyworld are largely absent. Regardless of how useful concepts such as storyworld may be for understanding narration in several media types, they are not transmedial enough to find their way into this study.

However, my intention is not only to put aside concepts that are too media-specific but also to embed the investigation of transmedial narration in some central issues of communication at large. Therefore, I will include elaborations on concepts of communication that actually go beyond the defining traits of narration but are essential for making sense of them. Hence, another purpose of this work is to put the issue of transmedial narration in a wide-ranging setting of transmedial communication.

Although I will strive for logical coherence and systematic rigor, and certainly apply many distinctions, I will also resist the tendency to form too rigid conceptual structures. Barbara Herrnstein Smith (1981) criticized the tendency in early narratology to form dualistic concepts (such as story vs. discourse). My own conceptual distinctions should be understood as ways of modeling the complexities of transmedial narration and developing suggestions for methodical thinking about media interrelations. Thus, I wish to avoid trying to define or postulate criteria for what narratives are as such or how narratives in different media types are actually, by themselves, related to each other. If pushed too far, these questions become rather pointless. Narration is a *perceived quality* that is always somehow grounded in certain media products, and sometimes very strongly so, but is ultimately evoked by the perceivers. Consequently, narrative transmedial interrelations are also, to a large extent, phenomena that emerge in the mind of the perceivers. Therefore, I will interrogate how narratives may be construed by perceivers on the basis of various sorts of media products. A crucial goal is to improve our understanding of how such perceived narrative qualities depend on both basic, material media traits and mental operations that may be either very subjective or strongly intersubjective.

But why bother about transmedial narration at all? On the most general level, it is important to be able to understand and analyze ubiquitous communicative phenomena such as narration simply because communication is so vital for the existence of human beings—and a proper understanding of the place of narration in communication at large requires a transmedial approach. More specifically, a transmedial perspective on communication and narration is necessary for creating links among more-or-less isolated research areas that would profit from cross-fertilization. A transmedial methodology makes it possible to compare, in some detail, how narration works in areas of communication that are, by routine, considered to be unrelated.

Furthermore, developed transmedial concepts enable careful investigations of how narratives are transmediated in all forms of communication in the whole society—from casual everyday communication to advanced political, artistic, or scientific communication—and what the consequences of such transmediations might be in terms of both added and corrupted significance. One vital media characteristic that may be distorted by transmediation, sometimes with immense implications, is truthfulness; coming closer to an understanding of these processes appears to be urgent.

Although it is certainly meaningful and necessary to also investigate media-specific narration, such endeavors will remain incapable of contributing to a broader understanding of narration and human communication at large as long as transmedial narration is not a point of reference.

Disposition

In the remainder of Part I "Drawing the Frame", narration is first put into the area of communication at large. In Chap. 2, I propose several general concepts for modeling communication and relate these to some influential psychological and cognitive concepts. After that, the stage is set for a transmedial definition of narration followed by semiotic and cognitive elaborations in Chap. 3. Chapter 4 explores the fundamental similarities and differences among media types to explain why different media types may narrate to different degrees.

Part II, "Scrutinizing the Essentials", systematically investigates the core characteristics of narration and some general forms of transmedial media characteristics that I find essential to framing narration. Chapter 5 suggests a methodical and profoundly transmedial way of analyzing narrators that are external and internal to narratives. Chapter 6 circumscribes the concept of event, central to narration, and Chap. 7 scrutinizes the equally fundamental concept of temporal relationships among events, proposing some distinctions that are vital for grasping media differences. In Chap. 8, the formation of internal coherence in narratives is illuminated from several theoretical perspectives. Chapter 9 proposes some analytical tools for understanding how communication in general and narration in particular can be truthful to what we perceive to be the actual world.

Finally, the brief Part III of the treatise, "Demonstrating the Principles", illuminates and roughly summarizes some vital concepts and ideas. Its single chapter (Chap. 10) includes four sections investigating narration in dissimilar media types: painting, instrumental music, mathematical equations, and guided tours. These studies elucidate the usefulness of the theoretical framework developed in the treatise and highlight the media similarities and differences that make narration a profoundly transmedial but nevertheless media-dependent phenomenon.

REFERENCES

Abbate, Carolyn. 1991. *Unsung Voices: Opera and Musical Narrative in the Nineteenth Century*. Princeton, NJ: Princeton University Press.

Abbott, Lawrence L. 1986. Comic art: Characteristics and potentialities of a narrative medium. *Journal of Popular Culture* 19: 155–176.

Almén, Byron. 2008. *A Theory of Musical Narrative*. Bloomington and Indianapolis: Indiana University Press.

Alpers, Svetlana. 1976. Describe or narrate? A problem in realistic representation. *New Literary History* 8: 15–41.

Altman, Rick. 2008. *A Theory of Narrative*. New York: Columbia University Press.

Arvidson, Mats. 2016. *An Imaginary Musical Road Movie: Transmedial Semiotic Structures in Brad Mehldau's Concept Album 'Highway Rider'*. Lund: Lund Studies in Arts and Cultural Sciences.

Barthes, Roland. 1977 [1966]. Introduction to the structural analysis of narratives. In *Image—Music—Text*, trans. Stephen Heath, 79–124. New York: Hill and Wang.

Berning, Nora. 2014. Narrative journalism from a transdisciplinary perspective: A narratological analysis of award-winning literary reportages. In *Beyond Classical Narration: Transmedial and Unnatural Challenges*, ed. Jan Alber and Per Krogh Hansen, 117–135. Berlin and Boston: De Gruyter.

Bordwell, David. 1985. *Narration in the Fiction Film*. London and New York: Routledge.

Bremond, Claude. 1964. Le message narratif. *Communications* 4: 4–32.

Brilliant, Richard. 1984. *Visual Narratives: Storytelling in Etruscan and Roman Art*. Ithaca, NY: Cornell University Press.

Brooks, Peter, and Paul Gewirtz, eds. 1998. *Law's Stories: Narrative and Rhetoric in the Law*. New Haven, CT and London: Yale University Press.

Campbell, Richard, and Jimmie L. Reeves. 1989. TV news narration and common sense: Updating the Soviet threat. *Journal of Film and Video* 41: 58–74.

Canary, Robert H., and Henry Kozicki, eds. 1978. *The Writing of History: Literary Form and Historical Understanding*. Madison: University of Wisconsin Press.

Chatman, Seymour. 1978. *Story and Discourse: Narrative Structure in Fiction and Film*. Ithaca, NY and London: Cornell University Press.
Cohn, Dorrit. 1990. Signposts of fictionality: A narratological perspective. *Poetics Today* 11: 775–804.
de Freitas, Elizabeth. 2012. The diagram as story: Unfolding the event-structure of the mathematical diagram. *For the Learning of Mathematics* 32: 27–33.
Doxiadis, Apostolos. 2012. A streetcar named (among other things) proof: From storytelling to geometry, via poetry and rhetoric. In *Circles Disturbed: The Interplay of Mathematics and Narrative*, ed. Apostolos Doxiadis and Barry Mazur, 281–388. Princeton, NJ and Oxford: Princeton University Press.
Eakin, John Paul. 2008. *Living Autobiographically: How We Create Identity in Narrative*. Ithaca, NY: Cornell University Press.
Elleström, Lars. 2014a. *Media Transformation: The Transfer of Media Characteristics among Media*. Basingstoke: Palgrave Macmillan.
Fludernik, Monika. 1996. *Towards a 'Natural' Narratology*. London and New York: Routledge.
Foster, Susan Leigh. 1996. *Choreography and Narrative: Ballet's Staging of Story and Desire*. Bloomington: Indiana University Press.
Gaudreault, André, and Philippe Marion. 2004. Transécriture and narrative mediatics: The stakes of intermediality. In *A Companion to Literature and Film*, ed. Robert Stam and Alessandra Raengo, trans. Robert Stam, 58–70. Malden, MA: Blackwell.
Giannoukakis, Marinos. 2016. Narrative in form: A topological study of meaning in transmedial narratives. *Organised Sound* 21: 260–272.
Goodman, Nelson. 1981. Twisted tales; or story, study, and symphony. In *On Narrative*, ed. W.J.T. Mitchell, 99–115. Chicago and London: The University of Chicago Press.
Gorbman, Claudia. 1987. *Unheard Melodies: Narrative Film Music*. Bloomington: Indiana University Press.
Grishakova, Marina, and Marie-Laure Ryan, eds. 2010. *Intermediality and Storytelling*. Berlin and New York: De Gruyter.
Hausken, Liv. 2004. Textual theory and blind spots in media studies. In *Narrative Across Media: The Languages of Storytelling*, ed. Marie-Laure Ryan, 391–403. Lincoln and London: University of Nebraska Press.
Hayles, N. Katherine. 2001. The transformation of narrative and the materiality of hypertext. *Narrative* 9: 21–39.
Herrnstein Smith, Barbara. 1981. Narrative versions, narrative theories. In *On Narrative*, ed. W.J.T. Mitchell, 209–232. Chicago and London: The University of Chicago Press.
Hirsch, Marianne. 1997. *Family Frames: Photography, Narrative, and Postmemory*. Cambridge, MA: Harvard University Press.
Hoffmann, Christian R., ed. 2010. *Narrative Revisited: Telling a Story in the Age of New Media*. Amsterdam and Philadelphia: John Benjamins.

Hünig, Wolfgang K. 1974. *Strukturen des Comic strip: Ansätze zu einer textlinguistisch-semiotischen Analyse narrativer comics.* Hildesheim: Olms.
Jenkins, Henry. 2008. *Convergence Culture: Where Old and New Media Collide.* Updated and with a New Afterword. New York and London: New York University Press.
Kafalenos, Emma. 1996. Implications of narrative in painting and photography. *New Novel Review* 3: 53–64.
Kramer, Lawrence. 1991. Musical narratology. *Indiana Theory Review* 12: 141–162.
Kress, Gunther, and Theo van Leeuwen. 1996. *Reading Images: The Grammar of Visual Design.* London and New York: Routledge.
Kutschke, Beate. 2015. Semiotische Grundlegung musikalischer Narration. In *Musik und Narration: Philosophische und musikästhetische Perspektiven,* ed. Frédéric Döhl and Daniel Martin Feige, 193–225. Bielefeld: Transcript.
Labov, William. 1972. *Language in the Inner City: Studies in the Black English Vernacular.* Philadelphia: University of Pennsylvania Press.
Lavin, Marilyn Aronberg. 1990. *The Place of Narrative: Mural Decoration in Italian Churches, 431–1600.* Chicago: University of Chicago Press.
Liu, Annie Yen-Ling. 2015. Text, topics, and formal language: Musical narrativity in Franz Liszt's *Prometheus* and *Tasso. Language and Semiotic Studies* 1: 139–160.
Lutas, Liviu. 2016. Storyworlds and paradoxical narration: Putting classification to a transmedial test. In *Narrative Theory. Literature and New Media: Narrative Minds and Virtual Worlds,* ed. Mari Hatavara, Matti Hyvärinen, Maria Mäkelä, and Frans Mäyrä, 29–49. London and New York: Routledge.
Mahne, Nicole. 2007. *Transmediale Erzähltheorie: Eine Einführung.* Göttingen: Vandenhoeck & Ruprecht.
McClatchie, Stephen. 1997. Narrative theory and music: Or, the tale of Kundry's tale. *Canadian University Music Review* 18 (1): 18.
Mildorf, Jarmila, and Till Kinzel. 2016b. *Audionarratology: Interfaces of Sound and Narrative.* Berlin and Boston: de Gruyter.
Mittell, Jason. 2014. Strategies of storytelling on transmedia television. In *Storyworlds across Media: Toward a Media-Conscious Narratology,* ed. Marie-Laure Ryan and Jan-Noël Thon, 253–277. Lincoln and London: University of Nebraska Press.
Nash, Cristopher, ed. 1990. *Narrative in Culture: The Uses of Storytelling in the Sciences, Philosophy, and Literature.* London and New York: Routledge.
Neitzel, Britta. 2005. Levels of play and narration. In *Narratology beyond Literary Criticism: Mediality, Disciplinarity,* ed. Jan Christoph Meister, Tom Kindt, and Wilhelm Schernus, 45–64. Berlin and New York: Walter De Gruyter.
Newcomb, Anthony. 1987. Schumann and late eighteenth-century narrative strategies. *19th-Century Music* 11: 164–174.

Nünning, Vera, ed. 2015. *Unreliable Narration and Trustworthiness: Intermedial and Interdisciplinary Perspectives*. Berlin: De Gruyter.

Nünning, Vera, and Ansgar Nünning, eds. 2002. *Erzähltheorie transgenerisch, intermedial, interdisziplinär*. Trier: WVT Wissenshaftlicher Verlag Trier.

Page, Ruth, ed. 2010. *New Perspectives on Narrative and Multimodality*. London and New York: Routledge.

Psarra, Sophia. 2009. *Architecture and Narrative: The Formation of Space and Cultural Meaning*. London and New York: Routledge.

Ribière, Mireille, and Jan Baetens, eds. 2001. *Time, Narrative & the Fixed Image/ Temps, Narration & Image Fixe*. Amsterdam and Atlanta, GA: Rodopi.

Richardson, Brian. 1988. Point of view in drama: Diegetic monologue, unreliable narrators, and the author's voice on stage. *Comparative Drama* 22: 193–214.

Rimmon-Kenan, Shlomith. 1989. How the model neglects the medium: Linguistics, language, and the crisis of narratology. *Journal of Narrative Technique* 19: 157–166.

Ryan, Marie-Laure, ed. 2004b. *Narrative across Media: The Languages of Storytelling*. Lincoln and London: University of Nebraska Press.

———. 2005. On the theoretical foundations of transmedial narratology. In *Narratology Beyond Literary Criticism: Mediality, Disciplinarity*, ed. Jan Christoph Meister, Tom Kindt, and Wilhelm Schernus, 1–23. Berlin and New York: Walter De Gruyter.

———. 2006. *Avatars of Story*. Minneapolis and London: University of Minnesota Press.

———. 2007. Diagramming narrative. *Semiotica* 165: 11–40.

———. 2013. Transmedial storytelling and transfictionality. *Poetics Today* 34: 361–388.

Ryan, Marie-Laure, and Jan-Noël Thon, eds. 2014. *Storyworlds across Media: Toward a Media-Conscious Narratology*. Lincoln and London: University of Nebraska Press.

Schnackertz, Hermann Josef. 1980. *Form und Funktion medialen Erzählens: Narrativität in Bildsequenz und Comicstrip*. Munich: Wilhelm Fink.

Schwanecke, Christine. 2012. *Intermedial Storytelling: Thematisation, Imitation and Incorporation of Photography in English and American Fiction at the Turn of the 21st Century*. Trier: Wissenschaftlicher Verlag Trier.

Steiner, Wendy. 1988. *Pictures of Romance: Form against Context in Painting and Literature*. Chicago: Chicago University Press.

Stern, Barbara B. 1994. Classical and vignette television advertising dramas: Structural models, formal analysis, and consumer effects. *Journal of Consumer Research* 20: 601–615.

Thibault, Mattia. 2016. Notes on the narratological approach to board games. *KOME: An International Journal of Pure Communication Inquiry* 4: 74–81.

Thompson, Kristin. 2003. *Storytelling in Film and Television*. Cambridge, MA: Harvard University Press.
Thon, Jan-Noël. 2015. Narratives across media and the outlines of a media-conscious narratology. In *Handbook of Intermediality: Literature—Image—Sound—Music*, ed. Gabriele Rippl, 439–456. Berlin and Boston: De Gruyter.
———. 2016. *Transmedial Narratology and Contemporary Media Culture*. Lincoln and London: University of Nebraska Press.
Walsh, Richard. 2007. *The Rhetoric of Fictionality: Narrative Theory and the Idea of Fiction*. Columbus: The Ohio State University Press.
White, Hayden. 1981. The value of narrativity in the representation of reality. In *On Narrative*, ed. W.J.T. Mitchell, 1–23. Chicago and London: The University of Chicago Press.
Wolf, Werner. 2003. Narrative and narrativity: A narratological reconceptualization and its applicability to the visual arts. *Word & Image* 19: 180–197.
———. 2004. 'Cross the border—Close that gap': Towards an intermedial narratology. *European Journal of English Studies* 8: 81–103.
———. 2011. Narratology and media(lity): The transmedial expansion of a literary discipline and possible consequences. In *Current Trends in Narratology*, ed. Greta Olson, 145–180. Berlin and New York: de Gruyter.

Open Access This chapter is licensed under the terms of the Creative Commons Attribution 4.0 International License (http://creativecommons.org/licenses/by/4.0/), which permits use, sharing, adaptation, distribution and reproduction in any medium or format, as long as you give appropriate credit to the original author(s) and the source, provide a link to the Creative Commons licence and indicate if changes were made.

The images or other third party material in this chapter are included in the chapter's Creative Commons licence, unless indicated otherwise in a credit line to the material. If material is not included in the chapter's Creative Commons licence and your intended use is not permitted by statutory regulation or exceeds the permitted use, you will need to obtain permission directly from the copyright holder.

CHAPTER 2

Circumscribing Narration

Abstract This chapter puts narration into the area of communication at large. Narration does not exist independently of minds but is a result of people communicating with each other. Therefore, some general concepts for modeling communication and the work of communicating minds are provided, partly influenced by Charles Sanders Peirce's semiotics. The importance of background knowledge for the realization of narration is emphasized and the issue of transmedial narration is related to some influential psychological and cognitive concepts.

Keywords Transmedial narration • Communication • Mediation • Representation • Gestalt • Image scheme

Having presented the map and calibrated the compass, I will now sketch the contours of a conceptual framework for communication. Narration does not exist by itself; it happens when we communicate with each other. Consequently, narratives and stories are not something that we find floating around independently but something that is communicated by minds. Before I define narration in Chap. 3 and then scrutinize transmedial narration, this chapter will present certain general concepts that I find helpful for modeling communication and the work of communicating minds. Without such a background, it is difficult to model narration and the work of narrating minds; the part cannot be properly understood without access to the whole.

COMMUNICATION, MEDIATION, REPRESENTATION

I start by postulating that communication should be understood here not only as communication among minds in general, but more specifically among human minds. This is simply because the capacities of human minds partly differ from the capacities of the minds of other animals. While recent research has revealed amazing cognitive abilities among several mammals and birds, there are still large differences. Although these differences can be bridged, making communication among different species possible and even widespread, a discussion of that subject is beyond the limits of this study.

To communicate is to share ideas, thoughts, notions, and understandings. I call these shared entities *cognitive import*. At least two minds must be involved in communication and, somehow, a transfer of cognitive import occurs between them. My suggestion is to speak and write about the *producer's mind* and the *perceiver's mind* to refer to the mental places in which cognitive import appears. First, there are certain mental configurations in the producer's mind; then, following the communicative transfer, there are mental configurations in the perceiver's mind that are at least remotely similar to those in the producer's mind. Clearly, an intermediate entity is required to make such a transfer possible. I suggest calling this intermediate entity a *media product*. A media product enables the complex transfer of cognitive import from one (or several) producer's mind(s) to one (or several) perceiver's mind(s). I have elaborated on all these notions elsewhere (Ellerström 2018a, b). It may be noted, for instance, that in certain media types, such as those called interactive, one and the same mind may have the separate functions of being both co-producer and perceiver of the evolving media product.

The media product must be somehow material, although not necessarily solid or even palpable. It needs to be a physical entity or process that has the capacity to trigger mental reactions through semiosis, meaning that it prompts the creation of cognitive import in the perceiver's mind; it acquires the function of a sign or a collection of signs. As the transfer of cognitive import among minds involves both material and mental aspects, I find it helpful to distinguish between two profoundly interrelated but discernible basic facets of the communicative process: *mediation* and *rep-

resentation (Elleström 2014a: 11–20). Mediation is the display of sensory configurations that are perceived by human sense receptors within a communicative situation. It is a presemiotic phenomenon and should be understood as the physical realization of entities (with material, sensorial, and spatiotemporal qualities, and semiotic potential). Consider the example of a person hearing certain sounds. Representation is a semiotic phenomenon and should be understood as the heart of signification (which is delimited here to how humans create cognitive import in communication). When a human agent makes sense of the mediated sensory configurations, sign functions are activated and representation is at work. Using the example, the listener may interpret the sounds she has heard as a voice uttering meaningful words.

My current emphasis is on the idea that both a presemiotic and a semiotic side exist to basic encounters with media. Whereas the concept of mediation highlights the material realization of the medium, the concept of representation highlights the semiotic conception of the medium. Although mediation and representation are clearly entangled in complex ways, upholding a theoretical distinction between them is helpful in analyzing complex relations and processes. In practice, however, mediation and representation are deeply interrelated. Every representation is based on the distinctiveness of a specific mediation. Furthermore, some types of mediation facilitate certain types of representation and render other types of representation impossible. As a case in point, vibrating air emerging from the vocal chords and lips that is perceived as sound, but not as words, is well suited for the iconic representation of bird song, whereas such sounds cannot possibly form a detailed, three-dimensional iconic representation of a cathedral. However, distinctive differences among mediations are frequently subtler and less easily spotted without close and systematic examination.

Thus, representation in communication is the creation of cognitive import through perception and cognition. To say that a media product represents something is to say that it triggers a certain type of interpretation. This interpretation may be more or less hardwired in the media product and the manner in which one perceives it with one's senses, but it never exists independently of the cognitive activity of the recipient—there are no signs unless there is a mind to activate sign functions. When something represents, it calls forth something else; the representing entity makes something else—the represented—present to the mind. This is to say, in terms of Charles Sanders Peirce's foundational semiotic concepts, that a sign or *representamen* stands for an *object*; Peirce's third sign constituent, the *interpretant*, may be understood as the mental result of the representamen–object relation (see for instance, 1932: CP 2.228–229 [c. 1897]). My concept of cognitive import created in the perceiver's mind in communication is an example of Peirce's concept of interpretant. However, the entire triad of sign constituents is actually part of a mental process, although both representamens and objects may be connected to external material elements or phenomena (see Elleström 2014b).

Whereas representation—the very essence of the semiotic—constantly occurs in our minds when we think without having to be prompted by sensory perceptions, it is also triggered by external stimuli. In this context, it is appropriate to focus on external stimuli resulting from mediation. In other words, representation also occurs in pure thinking and in the perception of things and phenomena that are not part of mediation, but the account of representation in this research is mainly limited to the creation of cognitive import on the basis of mediated sensory configurations—stimuli picked up by our sense receptors in communicative situations. The contention is that all media products represent in various ways as soon as sense is attributed to them. Hence, the media product can be understood as an assemblage of representamens that, due to their physical qualities, represent certain objects (that are available to the perceiver), thus creating interpretants (cognitive import) in the perceiver's mind.

I find these concepts indispensable for a methodical modeling of meaning-making processes in communication, and they will serve as a firm spine for delineating the concept of narration and, in particular, the transmedial aspects of narration. As the following chapters will demonstrate, these concepts make it possible to discern the fundamental similarities among media and still pinpoint where the essential dissimilarities are to be found. However, they should be complemented with some concepts that highlight the importance of background knowledge for meaning-making.

Background Knowledge, Virtual Spheres

As no mind is a static and isolated entity that is dependent only on its inherited characters, the concept of communicated cognitive import in the producer's and the perceiver's mind must be examined also with an emphasis on how minds are molded by surrounding factors. In addition to its innate basic capacity to perceive and interpret mediated qualities (discussed in more detail later), the mind is inclined to form cognitive import on the basis of acquired knowledge, experiences, beliefs, expectations, preferences, and values—preconceptions that are largely shaped by individual experiences of culture, society, geography, and history. It is clear that all this is immensely important for the outcome of communication. The perceiver's mind acts upon the perceived media product on the basis of both its hardwired cognitive capacities and its attained predispositions; evidently, the cognitive import that is stored in the mind before the media product is perceived has a significant effect—to various degrees—on the new cognitive import formed by communication.

This is a recognized phenomenon that has been extensively theorized in various ways and minutely scrutinized within theory of interpretation and other research areas. What I offer here is a complementary semiotic way of modeling how cognitive import in communication is formed by private and public environments. Although I focus on the perceiver's mind, the basic suggested principles are also relevant to the formation of cognitive import in the producer's mind.

I have already established that the representamens that initiate semiosis in communication come from sensory perception of media products. One perceives configurations of sound, vision, touch, and so forth that are created or brought out by someone and understood to signify something. They make objects (in the Peircean sense) present to one's mind—and eventually result in interpretants based on the representamen–object relation: it is these interpretants that constitute the cognitive import being communicated. But where do the objects come from? They clearly do not emerge out of nothing; they are drawn forth from earlier percepts, sensations, and notions that are stored in the perceiver's mind, either in long-term or short-term memory that may also cover ongoing communication. 'Earlier' could be a century ago or a fraction of a second ago.

In semiotic terms, the stored mental entities may be direct percepts from outside of communication, interpretants from semiosis outside of communication, interpretants from semiosis in earlier communication, or interpretants from semiosis in ongoing communication. This is to say that objects of semiosis always require "collateral experience" (Peirce 1958: CP 8.177–185 [1909]; cf. Bergman 2009) that may derive both from within and without ongoing communication. In other words, collateral experience may both be formed by semiosis inside the spatiotemporal frame of the communicative act and stem from other, earlier involvements with the world, including former communication as well as direct experience of the surrounding existence.

In line with this twofold origin of collateral experience, I distinguish between two intertwined but distinct areas in the mind of the perceiver of media products: the *intracommunicational* and the *extracommunicational domains*. In doing so, I emphasize a difference between the forming of cognitive import in ongoing communication and what precedes and surrounds it (Elleström 2018a, Forthcoming; related but divergent distinctions in cognitive psychology have been proposed by Brewer 1987: 187). I also find it appropriate to make a corresponding distinction between *intracommunicational* and *extracommunicational objects*, both of which are formed by collateral experience from their respective domains.

From a broad temporal perspective, the extracommunicational domain is clearly prior to each new intracommunicational domain created and should therefore be understood as the background area in the mind of the perceiver of media products. This comprises everything one is already familiar with. As it is a mental domain, it does not consist of the world as such, but rather of what one believes and knows through perception and semiosis. In other words, one's stored experiences not only consist of percepts as such but also of percepts that have been contemplated and processed by the mind through semiosis. This involves estimations and evaluations of encounters with people, societies, and cultures that are consciously or unconsciously accepted, put in doubt, or rejected. The extracommunicational domain includes experiences of both what one presumes to be more objective state of affairs (e.g., dogs, universities, music, and statistical relations), what one presumes to be more subjective state of affairs (states of mind related to individual experiences), and everything in between. Thus, it is actually formed in one's mind not only through semiosis and immediate external perception but also through interoception, proprioception, and mental introspection. Hence, the extracommunicational/intracommunicational domain distinction is very different from exterior/interior to the mind, world/individual, material/mental, and objective/subjective.

It is imperative to note that vital parts of the extracommunicational domain are constituted by perception and interpretation of media products. Thus, former communication is very much part of what precedes and surrounds ongoing communication. Together, non-communicative and communicative prior experiences form "a horizon of possibilities", to borrow an expression from Marie-Laure Ryan (1984: 127); the extracommunicational domain is the reservoir from which entities are collected to form new constellations of objects in the intracommunicational domain.

In contrast to the extracommunicational domain, the intracommunicational domain is at the foreground of the mind of the perceiver of media products. It is formed by one's perception and interpretation of the media products that are present in the ongoing act of communication. It is based on both extracommunicational objects (emanating from the extracommunicational domain) and intracommunicational objects (arising in the intracommunicational domain) that together result in interpretants making up a salient cognitive import in the perceiver's mind. However, the intracommunicational domain is largely mapped upon the extracommunicational domain. Rehashing Ryan's "principle of minimal departure" (1980: 406), I argue that one construes the intracommunicational domain as being the closest possible to the extracommunicational domain and allows for deviations only when they cannot be avoided. In other words, one does not question familiar ideas and experiences until such questioning is called for.

As the intracommunicational domain is formed by communicative semiosis, it may be called a *virtual sphere*. The virtual should not be understood in opposition to the actual but as something that has potential. Hence, I define the virtual as a mental sphere, created by communicative semiosis, that *has the potential* to have *real connections* to the extracommunicational. In other words, a virtual sphere may possibly represent extracommunicational objects indexically (indices being signs based on real connections); it may be truthful to the extracommunicational domain (this notion of truthfulness is further elaborated in Elleström (Forthcoming) and will be conferred in some detail in Chap. 9 in this treatise).

A virtual sphere can consist of many kinds of cognitive import. This could be anything from a brief thought triggered by a few spoken words, a gesture, or a quick glance at an advertisement, to a complex narrative or a scientific theory formed by hours of watching television or reading books. Depending on the degree of attention to the media products, the borders of a virtual sphere need not be clearly defined. As communication is generally anything but flawless, a virtual sphere may be very incomplete or even fragmentary. It may also include clashing ideas or inconsistent notions. As virtual spheres consist of cognitive import resulting from communication, they are, by definition, shareable among minds to some extent.

The coexistence of intracommunicational and extracommunicational objects results in a possible double view on virtual spheres. From one point of view, they form self-ruled spheres with a certain degree of experienced autonomy; from another point of view, they are always heavily dependent on the extracommunicational domain. The crucial point is that intracommunicational objects cannot be created *ex nihilo*; in effect, they are completely derived from extracommunicational objects. This is because nothing can actually be grasped in communication without the resource of extracommunicational objects. Even the most fanciful narratives require recognizable objects in order to make sense (cf. Bergman 2009: 261). To be more precise: intracommunicational objects are always, in some way, parts, combinations, or blends of extracommunicational objects. Even more precisely, intracommunicational objects are parts, combinations, or blends of interpretants resulting from representation of extracommunicational objects. For example, it is possible to represent a griffin (which, to the best of our knowledge, exists only in virtual spheres) because we are acquainted with extracommunicational material objects such as lions and eagles that can easily be combined. A virtual sphere may even include notions such as a round square, consisting of two mutually exclusive extracommunicational objects that together form an odd intracommunicational object. Literary characters such as Lily Briscoe in Virginia Woolf's novel *To the Lighthouse* are composite intracommunicational objects consisting of extracommunicational material and mental objects that stem from the world as one knows it. One cannot imagine Lily Briscoe unless one is fairly familiar with notions such as walking, talking, and eating; what it means to refer to persons with certain names; what women and men, adults and children are; what it means to love and to be bored; and what artistic creation is. Also, more purely mental extracommunicational objects may be modified or united into new mental intracommunicational objects. Objects such as familiar emotions may be combined into novel intracommunicational objects consisting of conflicts between or blends of emotions that are perceived as unique, although one is already acquainted with the components. For instance, one may already be familiar with the separate emotions of feeling affection and disgust and then, through communication, have these clashing sensations merged into what one perceives as a new intracommunicational object.

The question that then arises is, if all intracommunicational objects are ultimately derived from extracommunicational objects, how come virtual spheres, narratives and others, are often experienced as having a certain degree of autonomy? This is because they, either in part or in whole, may be perceived as new gestalts that disrupt the connection to the extracommunicational domain. This happens when one does not immediately *rec-*

ognize the new composites of extracommunicational objects. The reason why they are not *re*-cognized is that they have not earlier been cognized in the particular constellation or merger in which they appear in the virtual sphere. Several such disruptions lead to greater perceived intracommunicational domain autonomy. Even though intracommunicational objects are entirely dependent on extracommunicational objects, one could say that they emerge within the intracommunicational domain.

The relation between extracommunicational and intracommunicational objects may be even more complex than hitherto indicated. Intracommunicational objects that are perceived as new gestalts might, in turn, be part of more embracing gestalts that *are* recognized from the extracommunicational domain. A virtual sphere can contain representations of intracommunicational objects such as living trains formed by familiar extracommunicational objects such as 'man-made machines for transportation' and 'the quality of being animate and conscious' that together form a new gestalt. However, when living trains quarrel or fall in love with each other, they interact in a way that is directly recognized from the extracommunicational domain. The conclusion is that intracommunicational objects may be interspersed among extracommunicational objects in numerous, complicated ways.

In brief, then, virtual spheres are made of clusters of objects represented by media products; these clusters form cognitive import with a certain degree of internal coherence. This may be described as intracommunicational indexicality, indices being signs based on real connections; in this case, connections within a virtual sphere (the notion of internal coherence is developed in Elleström (Forthcoming) and will be dealt with in Chap. 8 in this study). I submit that narratives should be understood as *virtual spheres with certain features*, to be defined in the next chapter. As virtual spheres, by definition, may be communicated, it follows that they are intersubjective to a certain extent; they may be shared among several minds.

The advantage of such a conceptualization is that narratives can be neatly compared with other forms of communicated cognitive import; they are given a theoretical as well as pragmatic framework that enables methodical investigations of both the peculiarities and the commonalities of narratives. While narration is a communicative form that is specific and important enough to deserve special attention, it is, at the same time, only a variation of, and sometimes not at all clearly delimited from, producing virtual spheres in general. Furthermore, the concept of virtual sphere offers an instrument to relate narratives and other clusters of objects represented by media products to what we perceive to be the actual world and to the background knowledge of the perceivers in a nuanced way (see also Chap. 9).

It should also be noted that the concept of virtual sphere is compatible with the common narratological concept of *storyworld*. However, although the latter concept is defined in a variety of ways by different authors, it is clear that the idea of a storyworld is narrower than the idea of a virtual sphere: it mainly refers to the kinds of virtual spheres that may be evoked by certain kinds of artistic media types such as literature, motion pictures, and comics, characterized by the prevalence of represented humans that act and interact in clearly perceptible spatiotemporal settings (see, for instance, Ryan and Thon 2014).

Perception, Gestalts, Image Schemes

I have suggested that virtual spheres are utterly dependent on background knowledge, which in more technical semiotic terms may be called extracommunicational objects. I have also suggested that, even though virtual spheres are composed of already known objects, narratives and other virtual spheres are generally experienced as having a certain degree of autonomy and coherence. Both of these interconnected conceptualizations are compatible with influential psychological and cognitive theories. Gestalt psychology has long taught us that, whether we want to or not, we constantly structure sensory perceptions to make them coherent and intelligible. Early on, the leading gestalt psychologist Wolfgang Köhler established that "stimulation, as such, is completely unorganized". The result of the operation of the rules of "sensory organization", which aim to put related things together in gestalts, is very often "a kind of reconstruction of those aspects of the objective physical situation which are temporarily lost on the way between the objects and the sense organ"; therefore, this process is in no way absolutely reliable (Köhler 1929: 177).

Modern cognitive and neurological research also confirms what many philosophers have suspected: that our perception is always an interpretation of the external world. The stimuli that reach our senses are not in themselves systematically arranged patterns that mirror actual reality but are instead a collection of more-or-less separate stimuli that the brain, on the basis of inherited skills and acquired experience, puts together into a comprehensible unity; they become meaningful by receiving form. Some information is selected and some is neglected. In fact, perception "may have evolved exclusively for *extracting statistical* regularities from the natural world" (Ramachandran and Hirstein 1997: 453). Although it increases our chances of survival to believe that our sensations are immediate effects of perceived external matters, and it is indeed the external world that causes our sensations, it is not the *perceived* external world, the world we see and feel, that causes our sensations. The perceived item (not the item in itself, of course) is actually caused by our perception of that item. Thus, as Norman N. Holland concluded in his enlightening article on neurological research from the point of view of literary reader-response criticism, the item is a projection of our sensations (Holland 2002: 29).

Neurological research has also established the idea that separate pieces of information are given meaning when perceived as coherent form, as forcefully demonstrated by gestalt psychology. This idea can actually be related to the notion that background knowledge shapes all semiosis, including the formation of virtual spheres. Perhaps the most foundational sort of background knowledge consists of our experiences of being living bodies moving within and interacting with the surrounding world, including other living bodies. Mark Johnson famously demonstrated that, as a result of these profound experiences, our minds are embodied. His concept of image schemas, understood as "preconceptual gestalt structures" that are formed by bodily experiences and various sorts of perception, gives an account of how this particular kind of background experience actually permeates the ways we think and communicate (Johnson 1987: 74). The influential psychologist Jean Mandler, who more generally emphasized the importance of perception of the outside world, stated that "children become able to think, that is, to go beyond perceptual categorization to form concepts" because "the attributes of adult concepts can be derived from the primitives of infants". Perceptual categorization involves elements of "conceptual activity", which means that all of our earliest concepts are based on sensory experience. Mandler proposed that "perceptual analysis results in redescriptions of spatial structure in the form of image-schemas" (1992: 587). Thus, both Johnson and Mandler stressed the close connection between bodily experiences and thinking, and both used the term 'image scheme' to denote the idea that bodily experiences and perception deeply affect thinking and conceptualization.

My conclusion is that the concept of image scheme also involves an idea of coherence: our thinking strives toward coherence partly because it is, to a large extent, derived from bodily perception, which our minds strive to give meaningful coherent form because it is beneficial for our survival. Importantly, sensory perceptions are not the only phenomena structured by our brains. Cognitive formations, such as those in virtual spheres, are also structured to make sense—to fit schemes. Therefore, gestalt psychological principles should also be valid for stimuli that have already been cognitively processed into conceptions. Whether we want them to or not, our minds also form thoughts, ideas, and notions into meaningful, somehow coherent gestalts. We crave structure and sense and virtual spheres are offspring of such organizing mental activities. Thus, narration is an important example of our need and inclination to represent and understand the world around us as meaningful gestalts.

References

Bergman, Mats. 2009. Experience, purpose, and the value of vagueness: On C. S. Peirce's contribution to the philosophy of communication. *Communication Theory* 19: 248–277.

Brewer, William F. 1987. Schemas versus mental models in human memory. In *Modelling Cognition*, ed. Peter Morris, 187–197. Oxford: Oxford University Press.

Elleström, Lars. 2014a. *Media Transformation: The Transfer of Media Characteristics among Media*. Basingstoke: Palgrave Macmillan.

———. 2014b. Material and mental representation: Peirce adapted to the study of media and arts. *The American Journal of Semiotics* 30: 83–138.

———. 2018a. Modelling human communication: Mediality and semiotics. In *Meanings & Co.: The Interdisciplinarity of Communication, Semiotics and Multimodality*, ed. Alin Olteanu, Andrew Stables, and Dumitru Bortun, 7–32. Cham: Springer.

———. 2018b. A medium-centered model of communication. *Semiotica* 224: 269–293.

———. Forthcoming. Coherence and truthfulness in communication: Intracommunicational and extracommunicational indexicality. *Semiotica*.

Holland, Norman N. 2002. Where is a text? A neurological view. *New Literary History* 33: 21–38.

Johnson, Mark. 1987. *The Body in the Mind: The Bodily Basis of Meaning, Imagination, and Reason*. Chicago and London: University of Chicago Press.

Köhler, Wolfgang. 1929. *Gestalt Psychology*. New York: Horace Liveright.

Mandler, Jean M. 1992. How to build a baby: II. Conceptual primitives. *Psychological Review* 99: 587–604.

Peirce, Charles Sanders. 1932. *The Collected Papers of Charles Sanders Peirce [CP]*, Vol. 2, ed. Charles Hartshorne and Paul Weiss. Cambridge, MA: Harvard University Press.

———. 1958. *The Collected Papers of Charles Sanders Peirce [CP], Vol. 8*, ed. Arthur W. Burks. Cambridge, MA: Harvard University Press.

Ramachandran, Vilayanur S., and William Hirstein. 1997. Three laws of qualia: What neurology tells us about the biological functions of consciousness. *Journal of Consciousness Studies* 4: 429–457.

Ryan, Marie-Laure. 1980. Fiction, non-factuals, and the principle of minimal departure. *Poetics* 9: 403–422.

———. 1984. Fiction as a logical, ontological, and illocutionary issue. *Style* 18: 121–139.

Ryan, Marie-Laure, and Jan-Noël Thon, eds. 2014. *Storyworlds across Media: Toward a Media-Conscious Narratology*. Lincoln and London: University of Nebraska Press.

Open Access This chapter is licensed under the terms of the Creative Commons Attribution 4.0 International License (http://creativecommons.org/licenses/by/4.0/), which permits use, sharing, adaptation, distribution and reproduction in any medium or format, as long as you give appropriate credit to the original author(s) and the source, provide a link to the Creative Commons licence and indicate if changes were made.

The images or other third party material in this chapter are included in the chapter's Creative Commons licence, unless indicated otherwise in a credit line to the material. If material is not included in the chapter's Creative Commons licence and your intended use is not permitted by statutory regulation or exceeds the permitted use, you will need to obtain permission directly from the copyright holder.

CHAPTER 3

Defining Narration

Abstract This chapter concisely demarcates narration within the broad field of communication. The story, which should be understood as the scaffolding core of a narrative, is circumscribed as *represented events that are temporally interrelated in a meaningful way*. This definition is precise enough to be operable, yet general enough to work transmedially. After specifying a number of vital implications of the definition, these implications are elaborated in the context of some concepts in semiotics and cognitive science.

Keywords Transmedial narration • Narrative: Story • Represented events • Cognitive schemata • Collateral experience

Having outlined a general conceptual framework in the previous chapter, we are now in a position to drill down to the issue of demarcating narration within the broad field of communication. In this chapter I will suggest how narration can be circumscribed more precisely. Building on earlier research, I will first seek to formulate as precise definitions as possible of the concepts that are required to shape a transmedial understanding of narration. I will then elaborate on these defined concepts through an interrogation of some vital semiotic and cognitive ideas. Thus, the chapter will first narrow down the perspective, only to broaden it again.

Transmedial Delineations

Almost all definitions of narration and narratives in the literature are clearly related to each other. On the whole, then, there is little serious disagreement about how the central concept denoted by terms such as 'narration' and 'narrative' should be understood. The disagreements are to be found in those important details that make it possible to operationalize the concept in various ways. Those particulars are often more or less media-specific and hence, from a transmedial perspective, too peripheral to fit into a precise definition. Here, I will illustrate with a handful of succinct definitions from research on various media areas.

Writing about spoken language, William Labov specified a narrative as "a verbal sequence of clauses" that represents events: "we can define a minimal narrative as a sequence of two clauses which are temporally ordered", meaning that the represented events must contain at least one "temporal juncture" (Labov 1972: 359–361). The most media-specific elements here are clearly "verbal" and "clauses". Discarding them, the idea of at least two represented events that are temporally ordered remains. Working mainly with literature, Gerald Prince's most schematic description of a narrative says that it "may be defined as the representation of real or fictive events and situations in a time sequence" (Prince 1982: 1). This is already a functioning transmedial definition, although the notion of situation is perhaps not transmedially ideal. As will be demonstrated in Chap. 9, I also find the distinction between "real or fictive events" to be much too crude to be useful. Vincent Meelberg, who mainly works with music but with a pronounced transmedial approach, defined a narrative as "the representation of a succession of events that succeed each other in time" (Meelberg 2006: 39). This is also a fully functioning transmedial definition, although, on closer inspection, Meelberg's idea of representation turns out to be much too narrow as it excludes several media types from the realm of representation. Finally, Murray Smith, who also approached the matter transmedially, first suggested that "A narrative is constituted by a set of agents and events linked in a cause-effect fashion" (Smith 2009: 2). After some discussion about uncertainties, he excluded the concept of agents and stated that "Perhaps the most minimal definition would stipulate only that, in a narrative, events must be represented in time" (Smith 2009: 3).

I have no objections to such a conclusion, although naturally everything depends on exactly how one understands the concepts of representation, events, and temporal relations—and on how one frames these entities. My way of explicating narration is to conceptualize it in terms of communication and media products—the intermediate entities of communication among minds—and how one construes cognitive import on the basis of media products. I have already stated that narratives are virtual spheres with certain features, and this statement can now be qualified by adding exactly the indispensable features that we have recently approached: narratives are virtual spheres containing events that are represented in time. This means that the events are represented in such a way that they are understood to occur at different points of time within the virtual sphere, whether these moments are situated in the past, in the present, or in the future in relation to the creation of the representing media product. In line with much narratological research, I also argue that the events must be perceived to be meaningfully related—a notion that I prefer to keep rather open, given the multitude of cognitive operations available for us to make valid connections among things and phenomena.

I believe that these conditions are both specific enough to be practically useful and general enough to be broadly transmedial. Therefore, I propose defining a narrative as a virtual sphere, emerging in communication, containing events that are temporally related to each other in a meaningful way. Thus, the core of a narrative is exactly this: *represented events that are temporally interrelated in a meaningful way*. As the core consists of several elements, it might also be described as a scaffold. I also suggest that a whole virtual sphere containing such a core and normally also other media characteristics should be called a *narrative* and that the scaffolding core should be called a *story*. *Narration* should simply be understood as *the communication of narratives*.

From this, it follows that what we perceive to be the same story may be realized in dissimilar settings in different narratives. What we recognize as basically the same story can be narrated in different ways. For those acquainted with literature and film narratology, this conclusion does not come as a surprise. However, the nature of the sameness of stories has been debated, and here I prefer to take a pragmatic stance. I simply do not believe that there is a method of exactly delimiting the story of an actual narrative; virtual spheres are rather fragile mental constructs that cannot always be intersubjectively dissected. The philosophical difficulty of establishing whether stories in different narratives are "the same" or only belong to the same "story type" (Smuts 2009), for instance, is interesting but of little significance for understanding transmediality. I do not think that definitively establishing such issues is necessary or even possible outside the realm of copyright trials. While the complexity of actual cases of narration may be illuminated and partly disentangled with the aid of the theoretical distinction between narrative and story, there is not necessarily always a point in trying to establish exact borders. I would argue that boundaries between complete narratives and their scaffolding story cores might well be differently conceived depending on the perceiver's background knowledge and perspectives. What is crucial for transmedial research is that it is possible, common, and often useful to perceive that vital core constituents of some narratives—certain events being temporally related in certain ways—are more or less similar to vital core constituents of other narratives, possibly represented by other media types.

Given these conditions, it must also be emphasized that stories may either be construed for the first time by the perceivers of media products (on the basis of salient structures emerging as the narratives develop in the mind) or be recognized (from earlier encounters with narratives or events in the world). In other words, the story may be based either mainly on intracommunicational objects arising in the virtual sphere, or on extracommunicational objects in the form of already known stories or perceived events. In any case, stories have no autonomous existence, as one might be led to believe by certain narratological discussions. They are always results of some sort of interpretation performed by certain persons in particular communicative circumstances; never objective existences, but possibly intersubjectively construed (cf. Thon 2016).

The theoretical distinction between a complete narrative and its scaffolding core story is essential for understanding transmedial narration: stories are embedded in narratives and they may also, to a certain extent, be realized by dissimilar media. However, the surrounding narratives and the representing media products are often conflated in narrative theory and sometimes termed discourse (they are not conflated by Chatman, though; see 1978: 23–24). However, there are not only two levels here—called, for instance, story and discourse—but rather three (cf. Genette 1980 [1972] and Bal 2009 who also suggested three-layer distinctions, although quite different from mine; cf. also discussions of "three levels" in Meelberg 2006: 43–44; Thon 2016: 36). A full discussion of all suggested conceptualizations of the matter would lead me far off track, so here I will simply make clear some consequences of my conceptualization of narration so far, which leads us to recognizing these three levels.

- A media product with particular basic media traits and other formative qualities provides certain sensory configurations that are perceived by someone; these sensory configurations come to represent ...
- ... media characteristics forming a complete narrative with all its many specific details and features; furthermore, the perceiver comprehends that this narrative surrounds ...
- ... a scaffolding core, the story, consisting of represented events that are temporally interrelated in a meaningful way.

It should also be reemphasized that stories and parts of their surroundings in the whole narrative may often be realized fairly completely by several kinds of media. This is because many media types have the capacity, to some extent, to represent events, temporal relationships, meaningful relationships, and an abundance of other media characteristics. The story is normally only one of many transmedial media characteristics in narratives. The complete narrative of a certain media product may include a multitude of different media characteristics that may be more or less transmedial. However, as a rule, a story, consisting of the essential temporal structure of a narrative, is more transmedial than the complete narrative, although probably never wholly transmedial (cf. rewarding discussions of this issue in Gaudreault and Marion 2004).

Semiotic and Cognitive Elaborations

Brief definitions such as those in the previous section cannot stand alone; they must be entrenched in more comprehensive frameworks. I have already introduced and developed the frame of communication and the idea that narratives consist of represented events. In Peircean semiotic terms, this means, more specifically, as we have noted, that they are made up of represented objects that are construed such that they result in interpretants making meaningfully interrelated events present to the mind of the perceiver. To push the exploration of transmedial narration forward at this point, I must reemphasize that objects do not arise out of nothing; they depend on what Peirce calls collateral experience.

In this context, collateral experience is understood as collateral experience in the extracommunicational domain: what the perceiver of media products already somehow knows of or is familiar with. It may be experience of anything from simple entities such as water to complex processes such as how to build a house, or indeed knowledge of specific narratives. Collateral experience may also be understood as even more profound and omnipresent experiences, such as those emphasized by Mandler and Johnson: experience of common structures of perception and body activity. Their theories may be understood as suggesting explanations of pervasive cognitive processes that are also reflected in communication. Thus, the notion that virtual spheres are formed by extracommunicational objects, background knowledge, covers both inescapable, prevalent experiences, such as those emphasized by Mandler and Johnson, and more specific and individual experiences, such as memories of certain items and events in one's life.

Earlier narratological research has accurately highlighted the relevance of collateral experience in general and, more specifically, collateral experience of more or less essential parts of narratives. Emma Kafalenos has emphasized that the perceiver's background knowledge largely determines the construction of narratives (Kafalenos 1996). Marie-Laure Ryan has stressed the difference between narratives that, at one extreme are entirely "new to the receiver" and, at the other extreme, are utterly dependent upon "the receiver's previous knowledge" (Ryan 2004a: 14; cf. Groensteen 2013 [2011]: 25). In the same vein, Michael Ranta has argued that previous knowledge is indeed very important and, furthermore, that, in general, "pictorial media, when compared to verbal language, require recipients who are more active in the reconstruction of narratives" (Ranta 2013: 7).

As Peircean semiotics is preoccupied with fundamental cognitive capacities and functions that render meaning-making possible, I think it is well in agreement with modern cognitive science. The central concept of *cognitive schemata* can be understood as fundamental forms of collateral experience. To the best of my knowledge, film scholar David Bordwell was the first to apply cognitive research to narrative theory. He highlighted the fundamental role of the perceiver of narratives and emphasized that narratives are constructs that are dependent not only on the perceived qualities of the media products but also on expectations and hypotheses. In brief, the realization of narratives relies on cognitive schemata in the goal-directed perceiver's mind (Bordwell 1985: 29–47; these ideas were developed in Branigan 1992: 13–32; and, with the main focus on literature, in Fludernik 1996 and Herman 2002: 85–113; narratives are also seen as cognitive constructs in the transmedial narratology developed in Ryan 2006).

Cognitive schemata can be understood as cognitive blueprints that are used to efficiently deal with and make sense of new input from the external world, including input from communication. One could say that they are based on condensed forms of collateral experience; large amounts of experience of the world, again including communication, that are abstracted and generalized into schemata. For instance, after having cooked food many times, or having observed someone who has, a person is likely to develop some sort of cognitive schema based on the expected main events: first, one collects the primary products, then they are prepared, then again they are possibly heated or combined in some way, after which the meal is served and eaten. As with all schemata, this one is not absolutely accurate for all cooking, but it captures much of the essence of much cooking—and may therefore create expectations about how to proceed when preparing a meal. It is also clear to see that cognitive schemata like this may serve as material for narratives.

As one might expect, there is no consensus among researchers concerning the exact nature and function of cognitive schemata. In this context, I find it vital to emphasize the great diversity of cognitive schemata. As already noted, we have a plenitude of forms of collateral experience. By the same token, cognitive schemata, being based on collateral experience, must be understood as existing in a great deal of different forms. Our minds develop small and large schemata. Whereas some of them are more temporary and fade away, others stay with us for years or our entire life. We have schemata that concern trivial things and schemata that are related to matters of life and death. Some schemata evolve out of experience of nature, others build on culture, and yet others on both. There are cognitive schemata that are based on experience of mental entities and processes (such as intentional action; see Bundgaard 2007) and there are schemata that have developed out of collateral experience of material entities and processes. Schemata may be highly subjective or more or less intersubjective. Intersubjective cognitive schemata clearly facilitate communication.

Thus, perceiving *represented events that are temporally interrelated in a meaningful way* in a narrative is a cognitive process that depends on collateral experience and, more specifically, on cognitive schemata. Sensing interrelations to be meaningful is at least partially a question of being able to relate them to things that one is already familiar with.

REFERENCES

Bal, Mieke. 2009. *Narratology: Introduction to the Theory of Narrative.* 3rd ed. Toronto: University of Toronto Press.
Bordwell, David. 1985. *Narration in the Fiction Film.* London and New York: Routledge.
Branigan, Edward. 1992. *Narrative Comprehension and Film.* London and New York: Routledge.
Bundgaard, Peer F. 2007. The cognitive import of the narrative schema. *Semiotica* 165: 247–261.
Chatman, Seymour. 1978. *Story and Discourse: Narrative Structure in Fiction and Film.* Ithaca, NY and London: Cornell University Press.
Fludernik, Monika. 1996. *Towards a 'Natural' Narratology.* London and New York: Routledge.
Gaudreault, André, and Philippe Marion. 2004. Transécriture and narrative mediatics: The stakes of intermediality. In *A Companion to Literature and Film*, ed. Robert Stam and Alessandra Raengo, trans. Robert Stam, 58–70. Malden: Blackwell.
Genette, Gérard. 1980 [1972]. *Narrative Discourse: An Essay in Method.* Translated by Jane E. Lewin. Ithaca, NY: Cornell University Press.
Groensteen, Thierry. 2013 [2011]. *Comics and Narration.* Translated by Ann Miller. Jackson: University Press of Mississippi.
Herman, David. 2002. *Story Logic: Problems and Possibilities of Narrative.* Lincoln and London: University of Nebraska Press.
Kafalenos, Emma. 1996. Implications of narrative in painting and photography. *New Novel Review* 3: 53–64.
Labov, William. 1972. *Language in the Inner City: Studies in the Black English Vernacular.* Philadelphia: University of Pennsylvania Press.
Meelberg, Vincent. 2006. *New Sounds, New Stories: Narrativity in Contemporary Music.* Leiden: Leiden University Press.
Prince, Gerald. 1982. *Narratology: The Form and Functioning of Narrative.* Berlin: Mouton.
Ranta, Michael. 2013. (Re-)creating order: Narrativity and implied world views in pictures. *Storyworlds* 5: 1–30.
Ryan, Marie-Laure. 2004a. Introduction. In *Narrative across Media: The Languages of Storytelling*, ed. Marie-Laure Ryan, 1–40. Lincoln and London: University of Nebraska Press.
———. 2006. *Avatars of Story.* Minneapolis and London: University of Minnesota Press.
Smith, Murray. 2009. Double trouble: On film, fiction, and narrative. *Storyworlds* 1: 1–23.

Smuts, Aaron. 2009. Story identity and story type. *Journal of Aesthetics & Art Criticism* 67: 5–13.

Thon, Jan-Noël. 2016. *Transmedial Narratology and Contemporary Media Culture*. Lincoln and London: University of Nebraska Press.

Open Access This chapter is licensed under the terms of the Creative Commons Attribution 4.0 International License (http://creativecommons.org/licenses/by/4.0/), which permits use, sharing, adaptation, distribution and reproduction in any medium or format, as long as you give appropriate credit to the original author(s) and the source, provide a link to the Creative Commons licence and indicate if changes were made.

The images or other third party material in this chapter are included in the chapter's Creative Commons licence, unless indicated otherwise in a credit line to the material. If material is not included in the chapter's Creative Commons licence and your intended use is not permitted by statutory regulation or exceeds the permitted use, you will need to obtain permission directly from the copyright holder.

CHAPTER 4

Narrating Through Media Modalities

Abstract This chapter explores the fundamental similarities and differences among media types to explain why different media types may narrate to different degrees. Based on a general conceptual framework for analyzing communication and a specific definition of narration, certain basic traits of media products that are significant for both communication at large and narration in particular are pinpointed. These basic traits are described in terms of the material, spatiotemporal, sensorial, and semiotic modalities of media. This conceptual framework makes it possible to distinguish between different ways of categorizing media; the differentiation between basic and qualified media types makes it possible to explain the differing narrative capacities of media types in a more refined way.

Keywords Transmedial narration • Media modalities • Basic media • Qualified media • Sign types

Based on a general conceptual framework for analyzing communication and a specific definition of narration, it is now possible to pinpoint certain basic traits of media products that are significant for both communication at large and narration in particular. However important the surrounding factors of communication may be—discussed above in terms of collateral experience, gestalts, and schemata—it is ultimately the more inherent factors of media products that trigger the mind-work of communication and,

© The Author(s) 2019
L. Elleström, *Transmedial Narration*,
https://doi.org/10.1007/978-3-030-01294-6_4

to some extent, determine how and to what degree narration may be realized in various media forms. It is clear that one and the same perceiving mind, harboring a certain set of knowledge, experiences, values, memories, and schemata, will interpret different media products in very different ways even if they are perceived in comparable circumstances. This is obviously because the media products are unlike in various ways and because the divergences are highly relevant. In order to understand how narratives can be communicated by dissimilar media types, one must first understand the fundamental similarities and differences among media types and the extent to which these differences matter. Those are the issues to be explored in this chapter.

Degrees of Narrativity

We have already noted that media characteristics may be transmedial to lower or higher degrees. Transmedial capacities are molded by certain basic media traits, which means that different media characteristics may depend on different basic media traits. Narration is one of many transmedial media characteristics, and the question is to what extent narratives depend on certain basic media traits. This question cannot be answered in a straightforward and definite way for the simple reason that narratives, notwithstanding elaborate definitions, do not constitute a clear-cut group of virtual spheres. Furthermore, narratives that are realized by media products belonging to the same media type may differ greatly. The notions of event and meaningful temporal interrelations allow for varieties that are large enough to create a span of narratives, even within one and the same media type. It is therefore not self-evident that different narratives within one and the same media type depend on exactly the same basic media traits. Additionally, media types overlap extensively regarding their basic media traits, and it is not even certain that a certain media product can be classified successfully. In the end, one must realize that there is, on the one hand, a broad spectrum of individual virtual spheres that can be perceived as more or less narrative in partly dissimilar ways, and, on the other hand, a wide range of partly overlapping media types that have more or less narrative potential depending on their basic media traits.

Therefore, I, along with Seymour Chatman (1978), Marie-Laure Ryan (2006), Werner Wolf (2017), and many others (although these researchers are supported by different kinds of theoretical arguments) emphasize that narration is present in various degrees in different media products. This has become a broadly accepted concept within narratology. I also agree with the majority of researchers of transmedial narration that even if many media types can narrate, they cannot do it to the same degree; as Ranta put it: "narratives may be manifested in various genres or media, and meaning bearers of various kinds may be more or less narrative. Narrativity can thus be seen as a matter of degree rather than kind" (Ranta 2013: 3; cf. Herman 2004). Although the degree of perceived narration can sometimes, in the case of specific encounters with particular media products, be explained by surrounding factors of communication such as general background knowledge and cognitive schemata, it cannot in the case of overall narrative differences among media types (although media-specific background knowledge may self-evidently sometimes be crucial for perceiving narration in a certain media type). Whereas general background knowledge and cognitive schemata are relevant for the perception of all media types, they cannot explain why narration is realized differently in dissimilar media types. The differences in the kind and degree of narration in various media forms have their primary origin in more specific, basic media traits.

However, in order to track down basic media traits that allow for interpretations in terms of degrees of narrativity, it is not sufficient to consider only the traditional range of loosely demarcated media conceptions: literature, text, image, music, visual art, comics, television news, film, speech, and so forth. For instance, I would argue that it is not sufficiently precise to discuss literature as a narrative medium: there is a large difference between visual and auditory literature, and even if one sticks to visual, written literature, there are considerable differences among, say, a classical nineteenth-century novel, a postmodern novel, and a short poem. On the other hand, written, artistic literature has many basic features in common with other forms of visual, verbal media types such as pieces of journalism, personal letters, scientific articles, and even simple manuals. Furthermore, dichotomies such as text versus image and verbal versus visual are too vague to be operational. Even if they are specified, the notions of, say, a written, verbal text and a visual, two-dimensional image are very inclusive and incorporate several basic media traits that partly overlap (such as visuality). Thus, the dichotomy obstructs the clarification of relevant media similarities and differences. The equally widespread opposition between verbal and visual media types is simply a false and hence utterly misleading dichotomy. Whereas the verbal is related to semiosis—namely, the use of language and a specific way of making meaning through a specific form of signs (symbols)—visuality is a form of perception. The dichotomy of verbal and visual media types is equally warped as a dichotomy consisting of green cars on one hand and fast cars on the other.

To avoid such confusions, I advocate a more fine-grained and systematic way of describing and analyzing media similarities and differences. My contention is that media share basic traits that must be theoretically isolated in order to be clearly visible. To find out how narration can be understood as a transmedial concept, yet realized in partly different ways and degrees by different forms of media, one must get back to basics. Werner Wolf (2011: 170–173) took a step in that direction, but I will follow a model for intermedial relations that I have already developed (Elleström 2010). I propose that what I call modalities of media can be used as a framework for comparing narrative capacities. A modality shall be understood as a category of related basic and universal media features.

Thus, I suggest that all media products, without exception, can be analyzed in terms of four kinds of basic traits—four media modalities. As postulated earlier, media products are the entities through which cognitive import is shared in communication. The perception of media products is deeply entangled with cognitive operations that may broadly be called semiosis. I have already discussed this process of transferring cognitive import among minds in terms of mediation and representation; the presemiotic and semiotic. The concept of mediation highlights the material realization of the medium and the concept of representation highlights the semiotic conception of the medium.

The Presemiotic Modalities

Accordingly, three of the four media modalities should be understood as presemiotic, which means that they cover media traits that are involved in signification—the creation of cognitive import in the perceiver's mind—although they are not semiotic qualities in themselves. Thus, the three modalities are not *a*semiotic; they are *pre*semiotic, meaning that the traits that they cover are bound to become part of semiosis as soon as communication is established. The presemiotic traits concern the fundamentals of mediation, which means that they are necessary conditions for any media product to be realized in the outer world, and so for any communication to be brought about.

The three presemiotic media modalities are the material modality, the spatiotemporal modality, and the sensorial modality. Media products are all material in the plain sense that they may be, for instance, solid or non-solid, or organic or inorganic, and comparable traits like these—comparable *modes* of the modalities—belong to the material modality. It is also the case that all media products have spatiotemporal traits, which means that such products that do not have at least either spatial or temporal extension are inconceivable; hence, the spatiotemporal modality consists of comparable modes such as temporality, stasis, two-dimensional spatiality, and three-dimensional spatiality. Furthermore, media products must reach the mind through at least one sense; hence, sensory perception is the common denominator of the media traits belonging to the sensorial modality—media products may be visual, auditory, tactile, and so forth.

A thorough understanding of the conditions for mediation requires systematic attention to all three presemiotic modalities. It is clear that cognitive import of any sort cannot be freely mediated by any kind of material, spatiotemporal, and sensorial modes. To provide some rather obvious examples, complex assertions cannot easily be transmitted through the sense of smell, and it is more difficult to effectively transmit a detailed series of visual events through a static media product than through a temporal media product.

The Semiotic Modality

The fourth media modality is the semiotic modality that covers media modes concerning representation rather than mediation. Whereas the semiotic modes of a media product are less palpable than the presemiotic ones, and are in fact entirely derived from them (because different kinds of mediation have different kinds of semiotic potential), they are equally essential to realizing communication. The mediated sensory configurations of a media product do not transfer any cognitive import until the perceiver's mind comprehends them as signs. In other words, the sensations are meaningless until they are understood as representing something through unconscious or conscious interpretation. In other words, all physical objects and phenomena that act as media products have semiotic traits by definition.

By far the most successful effort to define the basic ways to create sense in terms of signs is Peirce's foundational trichotomy: icon, index, and symbol. These three sign types are defined on the basis of the representamen–object relationship and can be understood as fundamental cognitive abilities. Icons represent objects on the ground of similarity; they stand for something, they make some object present to the mind because of a perceived similarity between representamen and object. Indices stand for objects on the ground of contiguity or, more precisely, real connections. Symbols represent objects on the ground of conventions or, more generally, habits (1932, CP2.247–249 [c.1903]; Elleström 2014b: 98–113). The same object, such as a steam engine, can often be partly or fully represented by different kinds of signs: one may imitate the sounds and movements of a steam engine and hence form icons of it; one may point to a present steam engine or in other ways direct the attention to the smoke hovering over a railway track and thus create indices of it; or one may simply say 'steam engine' in order to produce a symbol of it. Importantly, not every perceived similarity, real connection, or habit necessarily leads to representation. For instance, one may note the visual similarity between two newspaper columns without construing one of them to be an iconic sign of the other. Again, signs must be understood as dynamic sign functions, not as static entities or automatic mental responses.

I take iconicity, indexicality, and symbolicity to be the main media modes within the semiotic modality, which is to say that no communication occurs unless cognitive import is created through at least one of the three sign types (icons, indices, and symbols). They are normally mixed in various ways. As with presemiotic modes, the semiotic modes of a media product offer certain possibilities and set some restrictions. Obviously, cognitive import of any sort cannot be freely created on the basis of just any sign type. For instance, auditory iconic signs (such as in music) can represent complex feelings and motional structures that are probably largely inaccessible to the symbolic signs of written text; conversely, written symbolic signs can represent arguments and the appearance of visual items with much greater accuracy than auditory icons. Obvious examples like these are only the tip of the iceberg in terms of the various (in)capacities of signs based on similarity, real connections, and habits. Therefore, communicative transfer of cognitive import through media products is made possible—but also profoundly limited—by the semiotic traits of the medium. Whereas these semiotic traits are not as definite as the presemiotic ones, they are always somehow anchored in the physical appearance of media products.

Therefore, I argue that a semiotic perspective must be combined with a presemiotic perspective. Communication at large, as well as the specific case of narration, is equally dependent on the presemiotic media modalities and the semiotic modality. What we take to be represented objects called forth by representamens or signs (separate objects such as persons, things, events, actions, feelings, ideas, desires, and conditions, and composite objects such as interrelated events in narratives) are results of both the basic features of the physical media product as such (the mediated material, spatiotemporal, and sensorial modes) and of cognitive activity (resulting in representation). While signification is ultimately about mind-work, in the case of communication this mind-work is fundamentally dependent on the physical appearance of the media product. Having said that, some semiosis is clearly more closely tied to the appearance of the medium, whereas other semiosis is more a result of interpretation, and therefore the setting of the perceiving mind.

Thus, the most fundamental restraining and releasing factors of communication are to be found in the basic presemiotic and semiotic modes of the media products. Many exceedingly complex factors are clearly involved when the perceiver's mind forms cognitive import. My proposed model highlights one cluster of crucial factors in particular: media products have partly similar and partly dissimilar material, spatiotemporal, sensorial, and even semiotic modes, and the combination of modes partly determines what kinds of cognitive import can be transferred from the producer's mind to the perceiver's mind. Songs, emails, photographs, gestures, films, caresses, and advertisements differ in various ways concerning their presemiotic and semiotic modes and can therefore only transfer the same sort of cognitive import to a limited extent. Consequently, their narrative capacities differ.

Basic and Qualified Media Types

Up to this point, I have discussed the notion of media types in an unspecific way. The analytical framework of four media modalities makes it possible to now conceptualize the categorization of media with some accuracy. Although each media product is unique, thinking species such as humans feel the need to categorize things so that we can navigate in the world and communicate efficiently. We also categorize media products and, as is often the case with classification in general, our media categories are usually quite fluid.

However, some categories are more solid and stable than others because they depend on less variable factors. Therefore, I find it helpful to work with the two complementary concepts of basic media types and qualified media types (Elleström 2010: 24–27). Sometimes one mainly pays attention to the most basic features of media products and classifies them according to their most salient material, spatiotemporal, sensorial, and semiotic properties. For instance, we think in terms of still images (most often understood as tangible, flat, static, visual, and mainly iconic media products). This is what I call a basic medium (a basic type of media product) and it is relatively stable. However, such a basic classification is sometimes not enough to capture more specific media properties of interest. Therefore, one qualifies the definition of the media type in question and adds criteria that lie beyond the basic media modalities. One also includes all kinds of aspects of how the media products are produced, used, and evaluated in the world, and how they are situated in geography, history, and culture. One may wish to delimit the focus to still images that are, say, handmade by very young people; that is, children's drawings. This is what I call a qualified medium (a qualified type of media product) and it is more fluid than the basic medium of still image simply because the added criteria are optional and more variable than those captured by the media modalities. For instance, it may be difficult to agree on what a handmade drawing actually is: should drawings made on computers or scribble on the wall be included? And when does a child become a young adult rather than a child? The notion of childhood varies significantly among cultures and also changes over time, not to mention the individual differences in maturity. Thus, the limits of qualified media types are bound to be ambivalent, debated, and changed much more than the limits of basic media types.

Basic media include classes like still images (solid, flat, static, visual, and mainly iconic media products), written verbal texts (solid, flat, static, visual, and mainly symbolic media products), moving images (solid, flat, temporal, visual, and mainly iconic media products), and spoken verbal texts (non-solid, temporal, auditory, and mainly symbolic media products). There are many basic media types that we have no proper names for in everyday language. Qualified media include classes such as political speech, music, instruction manuals, sculpture, television programs, emails, and news articles. As qualified media types may be qualified in many different ways, and as they are often requalified as time passes, they not only overlap in intricate ways but may also emerge, change, and fade away.

The distinction between basic and qualified media helps us realize that the concept of transmedial narratology is not as straightforward as one might think. Early in this treatise, I described the concept of transmedial narration, in its most general sense, as the idea that a multitude of different media types share traits that render them narrative capacities. Although still valid, this notion turns out to be more complex than expected. Investigating narrative capacities of dissimilar media types must include at least two stages, for the simple reason that there are *different kinds of media types*. Consequently, the distinction between basic and qualified media allows for a more methodical approach to transmedial narration.

This is what I suggest: Instead of immediately comparing a broad variety of different kinds of media types, such as the narrative potential of comics, written texts, computer games, literature, music, images, speech and gestures, and so forth—comparisons that tend to become rather specific—one should begin by comparing the basic media traits: what is the role for narration, if any, of the material, spatiotemporal, sensorial, and semiotic modes of media modalities? Such comparisons can be expected to result in a more fundamental and wide-ranging understanding of similarities and differences in narrative capacities among media types in general. This initial query, framed by the notion of basic media types, will be pursued in Part II of the treatise, where the core characteristics of narration are scrutinized. After such an investigation of those basic media traits, which brings together all media types onto a common conceptual platform, investigations and comparisons of qualified media types can be made. As qualified media types are much more restricted than basic media types, such comparisons are likely to result in a narrower, but also more detailed, understanding of similarities and differences in narrative capacities among media. This will be tried out in Part III of the treatise. Needless to say, only a very limited amount of exemplifying comparisons can be made there, although the instances are chosen to illustrate transmedial narration in a really broad spectrum of qualified media types.

The Overall Relevance of Media Modalities for Narration

Before finishing this last chapter of Part I, I will provide an initial overview of the role of media modalities for narration, as preparation for the more specific investigations in Part II. Although differences in modality modes are largely responsible for differences in kind and degree of narration in various media forms, examining them does not offer a convenient shortcut to full understanding. Consequently, this section will not provide any easy answers to the questions that are raised by transmedial narration. Thinking in terms of media modalities is not a quick fix. The basic presemiotic and semiotic traits are always embedded in complex surroundings, so they generally need to be analyzed in their interactions with each other and with additional factors. Nevertheless, modeling narration in terms of media modalities facilitates a methodical approach to the issue of transmediality. Having different material, spatiotemporal, and sensorial modes implies having partly dissimilar capacities for narration and, by the same token, the use of different sign types has consequences for narration.

The material modality is perhaps the least crucial category of media traits for determining narrative capacities. Solid media products such as written verbal texts, as well as non-solid media products such as spoken verbal texts, clearly have very high narrative capacity, as decades of intense research has demonstrated. Furthermore, organic media products such as moving human bodies, as well as inorganic media products such as dolls in motion, may form complex narratives.

The spatiotemporal modality is much more critical for narration. This is because the scaffolding core of narratives consists of represented events that are temporally interrelated. The key question then becomes the extent to which the representation of a temporal object requires a representamen with certain spatiotemporal qualities. There is not much to indicate that media products should have specific spatial traits in order to be able to narrate successfully. Moving human bodies and dolls in motion are three-dimensional and, indeed, very suitable for narration. Written verbal texts are two-dimensional, but also potentially superbly narrative media products. Spoken verbal texts emanating from a singular source are spatial only in a limited way, but are still well suited for narration.

However, there are some relevant differences between temporal and static media products. Moving images that are inherently temporal may effortlessly represent sequences of events and hence also elaborate narratives. This is not to say that the represented events are necessarily understood to be interrelated in precise accordance with the temporal unfolding of the media product. In contrast, still images are, by definition, static and are thus incapable of representing events that are inescapably perceived in a certain temporal order. This is not the same as being incapable of representing temporally interrelated events; it only means that the scope of possibly represented events is reduced (assuming that the size of the still image is not huge) and that the perception of possibly interrelated represented events is not strongly directed by the physical interface of the media product.

Nevertheless, the difference in spatiotemporal modes reduces the narrative potentiality of still images compared to moving images—at least if one considers media products constituted by single still images. However, it is possible to construe media products consisting of a whole set of still images. Whereas this does not in itself enhance the narrative capacity, it opens up for the use of a special kind of symbolic element, namely the convention of sequential decoding. Perceivers who have learnt to process parts of certain kinds of static media products in a regulated order may distinguish represented events in temporal sequences that are as stable as those produced by media products that are physically temporal.

This line of reasoning is also applicable to the difference between spoken verbal texts and written verbal texts: the distinction between temporal and static media products cuts through both images and verbal texts. Spoken verbal texts are temporal because the sensory configurations of such media products constantly change as time passes; written verbal texts are static because the sensory configurations of such media products remain the same from one moment to the other (unless, of course, the text is perceived while it is being written or is a part of a temporal, visual media product such as a film). This means that spoken verbal texts, just like moving images—given that a certain volume of temporal extension is allowed for—readily represent sequences of events and may therefore produce intricate narratives. In contrast, written verbal texts are normally static and if we think of written verbal texts in rough analogy with solitary still images—namely as consisting of single entities such as one letter or one word—written verbal texts are equally handicapped when it comes to representing events that are inevitably perceived in a certain temporal order. In the case of language, however, the convention of sequential decoding is so strong that written verbal texts are normally understood to consist of large sets of subordinate symbols that are bound to be decoded in a manner that is highly regular. As in the case of sequential decoding of still images, this may lead to the discernment of represented events that are temporally interrelated in a manner that is as stable as those formed by physically temporal media products. This is why so many researchers—misleadingly, I would argue—claim that written verbal texts are temporal. Such a conception obscures the difference between the physical appearance of representamen (the traits of the media product), the process of perceiving the physical appearance of representamen, and the virtual appearance of object (the traits of the virtual sphere).

Thus, the fact that all kinds of media are perceived in time has some bearing on the capacity of representing temporally interrelated events: conventionalized orders of decoding may strongly enhance the narrative capacity of static media types. However, this does not erase the substantial differences between inherently temporal and static media.

Sensorial modality also plays a role for the narrative capacity of media products. This is mostly because the senses (understood here as the external senses) are not developed cognitively to the same degree. Sight and hearing are our two most advanced senses, in that they are strongly connected to complex cognitive functions such as knowledge, attention, memory, and reasoning. This means that sight and hearing are both well suited for narration. It is no coincidence that virtually all examples of narration in this treatise have so far included either the visual or the auditory sensory mode.

However, this does not exclude the other senses. The faculty of touch may be used for reading braille, for instance, or sensing the forms of reliefs and three-dimensional figures forming narratives. It is also fully possible to consider series of interpersonal touches that form casual, narrative media products. Children playing and adults having sex may well communicate elementary narratives by way of sequences of touches that are performed and located differently.

I presume that it would also be possible, in principle, to construe language systems mediated by taste or smell. In practice, however, they would probably be rather inefficient as a speedy decoding of symbols requires quickly performed sensory discriminations. However, taste and smell can no doubt be used to create at least rudimentary narratives. A well-planned meal with several courses served in a certain order may be construed as narrative to the extent that tastes and taste combinations may be developed, changed, and contrasted in such a manner that gives a sense of meaningfully interrelated events. A series of scents may be presented in such a way that represents, say, a journey from the city through the woods and to the sea, including encounters with people and animals with smells that reveal certain activities.

The three main modes of the semiotic modality are iconicity (based on similarity), indexicality (based on contiguity), and symbolicity (based on habits). All of these semiotic modes are immensely important for the realization of narration. Among those more acknowledged basic media types that are commonly reasonably well defined and have accepted names in ordinary language, a majority are saliently dominated by iconicity or symbolicity. Most of the recent examples of potentially narrative media types can clearly be characterized by a semiotic hallmark. Verbal texts, whether they are visual, auditory, or tactile, rely heavily—although certainly not exclusively—on symbolicity: the conventional meaning of letters, sounds, words, and so forth. Moving and still images, whether they are visual, auditory, or tactile, are understood to signify primarily through iconicity, based on perceived similarities between representamens and objects. Although series of touches, tastes, and scents are hardly acknowledged as media types in common parlance, a case could be made for recognizing them as basic media types dominated by indexicality: real connections between the perceived sensory configurations and what they stand for.

Furthermore, indexicality is an especially important semiotic mode for narration because it creates both internal coherence and external truthfulness (see Chaps. 8 and 9). Early on, Roland Barthes used the notion of index to frame some features of narration, but within a conceptual framework that differs fundamentally from mine (1977 [1966]).

For the sake of clarity, I have tried to isolate the possible contributions of various media modes to narration. By highlighting modal differences, it is possible to discern media traits that contribute to the gradability of narration. However, media products are normally more or less multimodal—in very different ways—which makes the above generalizations fuzzier, the differences among media types more subtle, and the issue of transmedial narration more multifaceted. What the model of media modalities can offer is not so much a lexicon of transmedial narrative capacities as a methodical approach to examining narration in a wealth of dissimilar media products and media types. In each specific media product and media type, the present modes of the modalities add, in profound interaction, to the forming of virtual spheres and possibly narratives. In a certain media product, the various presemiotic modes all contribute to forming certain sensory configurations: a cluster of physical representamens that together come to represent—iconically, indexically, or symbolically—a certain cluster of objects that possibly forms a narrative.

Therefore, I support Karin Kukkonen's conclusion that "[i]f, with Ryan, we understand narrative as a cognitive construct, different modes in multimodal media work together to provide the reader with clues to fill gaps and formulate hypotheses" (Kukkonen 2011: 40). Importantly, however, I go beyond the rather coarse notion of mode used by Kukkonen and in so-called social semiotics in general: modes understood as text, image, gesture, and so forth. In the present treatise, multimodality is a more fine-grained concept that can be more precisely circumscribed as four kinds of multimodality: multimateriality, multispatiotemporality, multisensoriality, and multisemioticity. As already stated, it is more the rule than the exception that actual media products and media types have many modes of one and the same modality. For instance, media products that consist of both organic and non-organic materiality are multimaterial. Media products that are both spatial and temporal are multispatiotemporal. Audiovisual media products are multisensorial. Furthermore, many media are multimodal in several ways simultaneously.

Finally, most media products are multisemiotic to the extent that sign types typically work in collaboration. In an early article advocating the value of applying Peircean semiotics to the study of narratives, Robert Scholes suggested that "we cannot understand verbal narrative unless we are aware of the iconic and indexical dimensions of language" (1981: 205), and this is certainly true. Even though symbolic signs are clearly the most salient ones, verbal language does not work solely through symbolicity. In visual language, for instance, lineation, letter size, letter form, and empty spaces may create iconic meaning; in auditory language iconicity is often produced by certain sound qualities, intonations, rhythms, and pauses. By the same token, most media types signify through iconicity, indexicality, and symbolicity in combination, although they are typically dominated by certain kinds of sign functions. However, one can find instances of communication and narration characterized by such extreme multimodality that virtually all kinds of modality modes, both presemiotic and semiotic, are included.

REFERENCES

Barthes, Roland. 1977 [1966]. Introduction to the structural analysis of narratives. In *Image—Music—Text*, trans. Stephen Heath, 79–124. New York: Hill and Wang.

Chatman, Seymour. 1978. *Story and Discourse: Narrative Structure in Fiction and Film*. Ithaca, NY and London: Cornell University Press.

Ellestrőm, Lars. 2010. The modalities of media: A model for understanding intermedial relations. In *Media Borders, Multimodality and Intermediality*, ed. Lars Ellestrőm, 11–48. Basingstoke: Palgrave Macmillan.

———. 2014b. Material and mental representation: Peirce adapted to the study of media and arts. *The American Journal of Semiotics* 30: 83–138.

Herman, David. 2004. Toward a transmedial narratology. In *Narrative across Media: The Languages of Storytelling*, ed. Marie-Laure Ryan, 47–75. Lincoln and London: University of Nebraska Press.

Kukkonen, Karin. 2011. Comics as a test case for transmedial narratology. *SubStance* 40: 34–52.

Peirce, Charles Sanders. 1932. *The Collected Papers of Charles Sanders Peirce [CP]*, *Vol. 2*, ed. Charles Hartshorne and Paul Weiss. Cambridge, MA: Harvard University Press.

Ranta, Michael. 2013. (Re-)creating order: Narrativity and implied world views in pictures. *Storyworlds* 5: 1–30.

Ryan, Marie-Laure. 2006. *Avatars of Story*. Minneapolis and London: University of Minnesota Press.

Scholes, Robert. 1981. Language, narrative, and anti-narrative. In *On Narrative*, ed. W.J.T. Mitchell, 200–208. Chicago and London: The University of Chicago Press.

Wolf, Werner. 2011. Narratology and media(lity): The transmedial expansion of a literary discipline and possible consequences. In *Current Trends in Narratology*, ed. Greta Olson, 145–180. Berlin and New York: de Gruyter.

———. 2017. Transmedial narratology: Theoretical foundations and some applications (fiction, single pictures, instrumental music). *Narrative* 25: 256–285.

Open Access This chapter is licensed under the terms of the Creative Commons Attribution 4.0 International License (http://creativecommons.org/licenses/by/4.0/), which permits use, sharing, adaptation, distribution and reproduction in any medium or format, as long as you give appropriate credit to the original author(s) and the source, provide a link to the Creative Commons licence and indicate if changes were made.

The images or other third party material in this chapter are included in the chapter's Creative Commons licence, unless indicated otherwise in a credit line to the material. If material is not included in the chapter's Creative Commons licence and your intended use is not permitted by statutory regulation or exceeds the permitted use, you will need to obtain permission directly from the copyright holder.

PART II

Scrutinizing the Essentials

The issue of media modalities will, more or less explicitly, permeate the remainder of this treatise. There will also be a certain emphasis on the idea of story. Although the story is only one of many varying media characteristics in narratives, it is the common denominator and defining core: represented events that are temporally interrelated in a meaningful way. More precisely, then, the story consists of a set of connected media characteristics. Complete narratives may include many different media characteristics that may be more or less transmedial, but to keep the investigation focused it is necessary to emphasize the essentials. Therefore, Part II will scrutinize the notions of represented events, temporal interrelations, and meaningful internal coherence.

However, the core characteristics of narration cannot be completely isolated from the broader features of communication in which narration is always embedded. For that reason, the discussions of the essentials of the story will be supplemented with elaborations of two general forms of transmedial media characteristics that I find essential to outlining narration satisfactorily. Thus, I will start Part II with a broad conceptualization of communicating minds and end it with an investigation of external truthfulness in communication. Both of these areas have, to some extent, long been part of narratology, discussed in terms of narrators and fictionality. As I construe the notions of communicating minds and external truthfulness, however, they are essential issues for the whole area of communication, of which narration is only one, albeit an important part.

CHAPTER 5

Communicating, Narrating, and Focalizing Minds

Abstract This chapter affords a broad conceptualization of communicating minds, which is essential for framing transmedial narration. It also suggests a methodical way of analyzing narrators and narratees that are external and internal to narratives. Distinctions are made between actual narrators/narratees and overarching and embedded virtual (represented) narrators/narratees in order to be able to discern both transmedial and media-specific narrative features. Whereas all narratives by definition require actual narrators and narratees, it is sometimes helpful to construe overarching virtual narrators or narratees that are internal to narratives and help in making sense of them. Narratives can also hold embedded virtual narrators and narratees creating stories within stories. Narrators additionally act as focalizers, delimiting the scope of narration in various ways.

Keywords Transmedial narration • Actual communicator • Actual narrator • Virtual communicator • Virtual narrator • Focalization

There is an extensive literature on the issue of narrators, their nature, and their possible existence or nonexistence (a good recent overview with a transmedial perspective can be found in Thon 2016: 125–166). Although I have profited in general terms from this literature, which will not be extensively discussed here, I will in this chapter form a conceptual framework that is suitable for using in the setting of all forms of communication by all kinds of media—not only narration and not only media types where the use of language is salient. However, narration will be pinpointed as a special case in order to get us back on the main track.

Although my suggested typologies in this chapter naturally resemble earlier categorizations in several ways, they are more flexible, precisely in the sense that they work for all media types. Given that narratives are conceptualized as virtual spheres formed in the perceiver's mind, which means that they are not determined to have any certain characteristics except for those stipulated by the definition of a story, they also allow for a pragmatic approach to the issue of narrators. I suggest that fruitless quarrels regarding whether certain kinds of narrators need to be present in various media types can be avoided by emphasizing the virtual nature of narratives and the modeling nature of the proposed typologies; the distinctions to be made in this chapter correspond to possible ways of construing narratives rather than to definite traits of narratives.

I will start by briefly presenting the contours and essential features of this conceptual framework and then discuss parts of it in some detail. This requires reemphasizing some general concepts that I have already introduced in this treatise. In Chap. 2 I distinguished between the intra- and extracommunicational domains and emphasized that they are utterly entwined but nevertheless dissimilar areas in the mind of the perceiver of media products. The point is to mark out a difference between the forming of cognitive import in ongoing communication and what precedes and surrounds it in the form of cognitive import stored in the mind. I call the intracommunicational domain, formed by communicative semiosis, a virtual sphere. Narratives are virtual spheres.

Regarding the extracommunicational domain, I have noted that vital parts of it are constituted by perception and interpretation of media products; previous communication is very much part of the background of ongoing communication. Thus, it may be said that the extracommunicational domain, the mental realm that precedes and surrounds the virtual sphere being formed in ongoing communication, consists of two complementary spheres: *other virtual spheres* (former interpretive results of communication) and what I propose to call the *perceived actual sphere*. The perceived actual sphere consists of earlier percepts outside of communication and interpretants resulting from semiosis triggered by these percepts. Every instance of communication is dependent on the experience of earlier encounters with things and phenomena in the world that have not been communicated by other minds. In summary, the perceived actual sphere is formed in one's mind through semiosis, immediate external perception, and also interoception, proprioception, and mental introspection.

Communicating and Narrating Minds

In Chap. 2 I also initially described communication in terms of a transfer of cognitive import between at least two minds, the producer's mind and the perceiver's mind, with the aid of an intermediate entity: the media product. After such a communicative transfer, there are mental configurations in the perceiver's mind—a virtual sphere—that to some extent are similar to those in the producer's mind. Acknowledging the presence of at least one producer's and one perceiver's mind in human communication is the starting point of the following distinctions among different kinds of communicating minds; distinctions that are vital for discerning some intricate conceptual structures of communication at large.

Before getting into details, I will present an overview of my proposed typologies in the form of two embryonic lists. The first is an inventory of different forms of communicating minds:

- A perceived actual communicating mind that is the actual producer of a media product = an *actual communicator*
- A perceived actual communicating mind that is the actual perceiver of a media product = an *actual communicatee*
- An overarching virtual communicating mind that is the producer of overarching communication = an *overarching virtual communicator*
- An overarching virtual communicating mind that is the perceiver of overarching communication = an *overarching virtual communicatee*
- An embedded virtual communicating mind that is the producer of embedded communication = an *embedded virtual communicator*
- An embedded virtual communicating mind that is the perceiver of embedded communication = an *embedded virtual communicatee*
- And so on; multiple layers of communication embedded in embedded communication.

The second list is a catalog of narrative minds. It is identical to the first list, except that communication in general is replaced with the special case of narration, meaning communication including stories:

- A perceived actual communicating mind that is the actual producer of a narrative media product = an *actual narrator*
- A perceived actual communicating mind that is the actual perceiver of a narrative media product = an *actual narratee*
- An overarching virtual communicating mind that is the producer of overarching narration = an *overarching virtual narrator*
- An overarching virtual communicating mind that is the perceiver of overarching narration = an *overarching virtual narratee*
- An embedded virtual communicating mind that is the producer of embedded narration = an *embedded virtual narrator*
- An embedded virtual communicating mind that is the perceiver of embedded narration = an *embedded virtual narratee*
- And so on; multiple layers of narration embedded in embedded narration.

As narration is a transmedial form of communication, the terms 'narrator' and 'narratee', precisely as the terms 'communicator' and 'communicatee', shall be understood to refer to comprehensive communicative concepts useful for disentangling a range of functions and levels in narration in effectively all (not only verbal) media types.

I will now comment on each of these forms of communicative and narrative minds and explain their interrelations and why I think they are useful for conceptualizing certain aspects of communication in general and narration in particular.

A perceived actual communicating mind that is the actual producer of a media product = an actual communicator. If communication is at hand, a producer's mind is, by definition, present, at least initially. The producer's mind is responsible for the creation of a media product that may be perceived by some other mind either directly, as in face-to-face communication, or later, as when one watches an old movie. I suggest that a brief and simple term for this entity may be 'actual communicator'. However, it is more specifically a communicating mind that must be understood to stem, more or less directly, from a perceived actual sphere. Hence, it is *perceived* to be actual, which means that there will always necessarily remain some epistemological doubts regarding its actuality. In face-to-face communication, the perceiver is close to the producer's mind, in both time and space. Hence, the immediate perception of the activities of the body holding the producer's mind becomes part of the perceived actual sphere. In the case of watching an old movie, the perceiver is normally at a spatiotemporal distance from the producer's mind. Consequently, the mind of the producer (the actual communicator) may well be known to the perceiver only indirectly, perhaps through earlier communication. In other words, the perceived actual communicating mind stems from other virtual spheres (that always rely, to some extent, on perceived actual spheres). In any case, actual communicators are by definition parts of the extracommunicational domain. A media product may be produced by either one actual communicator (like speech) or several actual communicators (like most movies).

A perceived actual communicating mind that is the actual producer of a narrative media product = an actual narrator. All that was said above regarding actual communicators can be specified in terms of 'actual narrators'. In brief: if narration is at hand, a mind producing the narrative media product must exist; there is, by definition, at least one actual narrator emanating from the extracommunicational domain.

A perceived actual communicating mind that is the actual perceiver of a media product = an actual communicatee. Just as communication (as I define it) requires a producer's mind, it also requires a perceiver's mind. The perceiver's mind perceives the media product produced by the producer's mind and forms a virtual sphere through the mediation and representation of this media product. 'Actual communicatee' is a straightforward term for this entity. Although it may seem a bit strange, the actual communicatee is also, like the actual communicator, a perceived actual communicating mind: the mind that perceives a media product has an awareness and understanding of itself and this self-understanding stems from what precedes and surrounds ongoing communication: the extracommunicational domain. Thus, a mind that perceives and makes sense of a media product does so on the background of having perceived and made sense of, among other things, itself—immediately or mediated through earlier communication. Therefore, an actual communicatee is more precisely a *perceived* actual communicating mind, again necessarily tinted by epistemological doubts regarding its nature and actuality. A media product may be perceived by either one actual communicatee (like someone receiving a nudge indicating which direction she should go) or several actual communicatees (like many people listening to the same talk).

A perceived actual communicating mind that is the actual perceiver of a narrative media product = an actual narratee. Again there is no need to repeat what has already been stated about the actual communicatee. What might be termed 'actual narratees' are the same as actual communicatees, except that they are more specifically involved in narration. If narration is at hand, at least one actual narratee perceiving the narrative media product must exist.

An overarching virtual communicating mind that is the producer of overarching communication = an overarching virtual communicator. Communicators are minds that make communication possible by producing media products. In virtual spheres, however, communicators are virtual; they are representations of minds forming media products with semiotic qualities. A perceiver of a media product, an actual communicatee, who for various reasons has no knowledge of, access to, or interest in the actual communicator, is likely to form a virtual sphere that includes a construed overarching virtual communicating mind that is the producer of overarching communication—in brief, an 'overarching virtual communicator'—that helps in making the virtual sphere comprehensible. Otherwise, it might be difficult to make sense of media products whose producers are anonymous. Hence, the craving for internal coherence, for gestalt, can be satisfied with the aid of a construed overarching virtual communicator: odd details, vague connections, and apparent inconsistencies may be knitted together through the idea of a virtual communicating mind having certain ideas, peculiarities, purposes, unconscious drives, or ironic inclinations. Overarching virtual communicators may also be needed when perceiving media products formed collectively by several actual communicators and trying to understand the resulting virtual sphere as somehow consistent.

By definition, a virtual sphere can have only one overarching virtual communicator. As soon as one thinks in terms of several virtual communicators, they are automatically subordinated to either an overarching virtual communicator or an actual communicator. Whereas at least one actual communicator is needed to bring about communication, the overarching virtual communicator is an optional entity that can be conjured up in the virtual sphere to make sense of it. Although it emerges within the intracommunicational domains, it may well be very similar to communicating minds in the extracommunicational domain, such as the actual communicator. This is because, as noted earlier, all intracommunicational objects, including overarching virtual communicators, are ultimately made up of parts, combinations, or blends of extracommunicational objects.

The idea of an overarching virtual communicator accords well with what has long been known in literary theory as "implied author" (Booth 1961) and what in film studies is sometimes referred to as "voice" or "hypothetical filmmaker" (Alber 2010), although different authors construe these latter concepts in different ways. There have also been many philosophical discussions regarding the rather awkward question of the possibly factual existence of this kind of entity in various media (see Diehl 2009). In any case, the concept of overarching virtual communicator is fundamentally transmedial. This is because overarching virtual communicators are only indirectly represented by the sensory configurations of the media products, so to speak; they are formed in a later stage of the chains of semiosis and therefore independent of the modality modes of the media products.

An overarching virtual communicating mind that is the producer of overarching narration = an overarching virtual narrator. Narration is communication including narratives, and narrators are minds that make this possible by producing narrative media products. An 'overarching virtual narrator'—a brief term for an overarching virtual communicating mind that is the producer of overarching narration—should be understood in analogy with the concept of an overarching virtual communicator, except that an overarching virtual narrator is obviously relevant in the case of narration. Nothing much needs to be added here, except a brief terminological comment. As the term 'narrator' has been used mainly for media types including verbal language, the term 'monstrator' has been suggested for the realm of visual iconic media (Gaudreault 2009 [1988]). Although this term stands for a concept that corresponds quite well with the concept of overarching virtual narrator, it would be unfeasible to use different terms for all basic media types that harbor narratives. For that reason, I stick to the term (actual or virtual) 'narrator' and postulate that it should be understood to stand for a transmedial concept.

An overarching virtual communicating mind that is the perceiver of overarching communication = an overarching virtual communicatee. While a perceiver of a media product (an actual communicatee) may have no knowledge of, access to, or interest in the actual communicator, an actual communicatee must be supposed to be aware of and have a certain amount of control of herself. Thus, there is no need to involve an overarching virtual communicating mind that perceives the overarching communication—an 'overarching virtual communicatee'—because the actual communicatee is out of reach. However, an overarching virtual communicatee may, just like an overarching virtual communicator, be helpful for making the virtual sphere comprehensible. In cases where the actual communicatee has a sense of not being an adequate perceiver at all, or when she believes that only parts of what is being communicated is graspable, it may be useful or even necessary to construe a virtual sphere including an overarching virtual communicatee. It is about construing an ideal perceiver's mind that might be able to grasp the entirety in a better way than the actual communicatee and hence achieve fuller understanding and better coherence (the concept of overarching virtual communicatee is a transmedial variation of what is known in literary theory as "implied reader" [Booth 1961]). In other words: the overarching virtual communicatee is the type of actual communicatees that is best suited for perceiving the media product. This ideal type of communicatee is something that may emerge within the virtual sphere as a result of the thought activity of the actual communicatee. Sometimes it is superfluous. As the concept of overarching virtual communicator, the concept of overarching virtual communicatee is profoundly transmedial and does not rely on the modality modes of the media products.

An overarching virtual communicating mind that is the perceiver of overarching narration = an overarching virtual narratee. The 'overarching virtual narratee' is a variation of the overarching virtual communicatee, of which nothing more must be said except that the exploration of narratees at different levels in literature was pioneered by Prince (1982: 16–26) in a way that has inspired this account.

An embedded virtual communicating mind that is the producer of embedded communication = an embedded virtual communicator. It is common for communication to be about communication. When talking to each other, one may mention other people who have said things or communicated them in other ways. Still images may depict acts of communication such as speaking, writing, drawing, or gesticulating. In all of these cases, one infers that communicating minds are involved in what is being represented. When seeing a still image of a writing person, for instance, one considers that the represented person must have a mind—a virtual mind, of course—that directs the writing performed by the directly represented body. In a case like this, the virtual sphere being formed by the perception of the static, visual, and iconic media product includes an embedded virtual communicating mind that is the producer of embedded communication; or, more succinctly, an 'embedded virtual communicator'. Virtual communicators like these are embedded, not overarching, because they only constitute smaller or larger parts of the virtual sphere, in contrast to overarching virtual communicators that have bearing on the totality of the virtual sphere. Although embedded virtual communicators, like overarching virtual communicators, emerge within the intracommunicational domains, they may more or less resemble minds in the extracommunicational domain. A virtual sphere may contain no, one, or several embedded virtual communicators.

An embedded virtual communicating mind that is the producer of embedded narration = an embedded virtual narrator. The 'embedded virtual narrator' is a special case of the embedded virtual communicator. It must be noted that literary theory in particular has come up with a multitude of terms and concepts that connect to the discussions here, although they are too media-specific to be relevant for a treatise on transmedial narration.

An embedded virtual communicating mind that is the perceiver of embedded communication = an embedded virtual communicatee. As already stated, it is common for communication to be about communication, and of course it is not only communicators, but also communicatees, that can be represented in communication. To reformulate the previous examples: When talking to each other, people may mention other people having listened to, seen, or in other ways perceived media products. Still images may depict acts of communication such as speaking, writing, drawing, or gesticulating, but also people listening to, sensing, or watching various media products, and we must then infer that these represented people have virtual minds that process the perceived sensory configurations. In alignment with embedded virtual communicators, a virtual sphere may harbor none, one, or several 'embedded virtual communicatees'.

An embedded virtual communicating mind that is the perceiver of embedded narration = an embedded virtual narratee. 'Embedded virtual narratees' are nothing more or less than specific forms of embedded virtual communicatees.

And so on; multiple layers of communication or narration embedded in embedded communication or narration. Continuing these lines of reasoning, embedded communication and narration may embed further layers of communication and narration. Communication or narration embedded in embedded communication or narration follow the same principles as communication or narration that is simply embedded in communication or narration. However, in contrast to overarching virtual communicators, communicatees, narrators, and narratees, embedded virtual communicators, communicatees, narrators, and narratees are to some extent sensitive to modality modes and therefore not fully transmedial.

Media types involving sophisticated systems of symbols, such as media including visual, auditory, or tactile verbal language, may easily represent infinite layers of embedded communication: 'Sarah said that she had read in a book that scientists claim that people who eat much sugar report that ....' Also, media types involving visual icons (whether fully spatiotemporal or three- or two-dimensionally spatial) have great potential for representing several layers of embedded communication. We have all seen images of people creating images of people creating images of people creating images *ad infinitum*. However, it is not as easy for these iconic media types to represent several layers of embedded narration if they are not temporal. Moving images may readily represent events in succession that include narrative events, such as when we see a story about someone going to the cinema, buying tickets, and then watching a movie about someone going to her desk, sharpening a pen, thinking a while, and then writing a letter about a friend who has traveled to Indonesia and fallen in love—and so forth. Still images, on the other hand, are less adequate for representing temporal interrelations being represented within other temporal interrelations, although it is certainly not impossible, especially if the perceiver's background knowledge is explored. In the case of media types that are recognized as potentially narrative only in a more elementary manner—such as a meal where the interrelated events consist of tastes and taste combinations that are developed and contrasted—the idea of representing embedded narratives offers even more resistance due to the limited amount of complex cognitive functions connected to the gustatory sense. As a rule of thumb, I propose that embedded narration is even more media-sensitive than narration as such, and that the deeper down in embedded narrative layers one goes, the less transmedial it all becomes.

Focalizing Minds

For a long time, narratology has, for good reasons, scrutinized concepts such as perspective and point of view and in numerous ways related them to narration and narrators. The related concept of focalization was first investigated by Gérard Genette in written literature (1980 [1972]: 186) and was later explored by, among many others, François Jost in film (2004), Kai Mikkonen in comics (2011), and Jonathan Hensher in still images (2016). There is an extensive literature on the entangled issues of perspective, point of view, focalization, and their interrelations (for a recent overview with a transmedial perspective, see Thon 2016: 223–264).

Focalization is variously conceptualized in terms of agency or functions that somehow delimit narratives and parts of narratives: not everything is seen, heard, or conveyed in a certain narrative. The scope of narratives can hence be understood to be restricted by one or several focalizers. Although originating from literary theory, focalization is actually a profoundly transmedial concept that, I believe, must be tightly connected to the concept of communicating and narrating minds.

It is often noted that the term 'focalization' has certain visual connotations. It is "based on the visual metaphor of a lens through which one can take things, characters, actions in the storyworld into 'focus'. It seems that a media-sensitive narratology has to revise this concept to accommodate all the other sense perceptions, too" (Mildorf and Kinzel 2016a: 14). While it is vital to revise the concept so that it clearly covers all forms of sense perceptions, this does not necessarily include revising the term. Several new terms have actually been coined for focalization of other sense perceptions than the visual, but I think it is untenable to use different terms for each different sense being involved, just as it is untenable to use different terms for narration and narrators in different media types. Such a practice would make transmedial terminology acutely overloaded and transmedial research unnecessarily cumbersome. As the term 'focus' is far from exclusive to the visual domain—it is broadly used for denoting points of convergence, attention, or action in a wide array of sensorial and cognitive domains—I find the term 'focalization' useful for transmedial narratology. Therefore, I prefer to continue talking about focus, focalizing, and focalization in all media types instead of introducing a broad range of new media-specific terms.

However, the concept of focalization is also highly useful outside the area of narration. For that reason, I define focalization as a main feature of communication at large. All virtual spheres are demarcated in various ways. The notion of actual and virtual communicators always communicating everything they perceive and know is clearly absurd, so it must be concluded that communicators of all kinds are generally also focalizers to some extent (pace Genette and despite the broad range of knowledge of so-called omniscient narrators). In order to cover the complex field of possible restrictions of what is being communicated, it is also vital to emphasize that focalization concerns not only restrictions on the communication of all kinds of sensory perceptions but also restrictions on all kinds of knowledge, thoughts, ideas, and values. As the awareness of sensory perception and cognition takes place in minds, it is minds that have the ability to select what is to be communicated; therefore, focalization must be performed by focalizing minds.

Focalization is an essential and unavoidable aspect of communication in general. As communication on all levels is entirely dependent on minds, from the actual communicators and communicatees to embedded virtual communicators and communicatees, focalization is located in minds on the different levels that have been described in this chapter. The actual communicator determines—consciously or unconsciously—certain frames of what to be communicated. When construing the virtual sphere, the actual communicatee furthermore interprets the communicated in terms of virtual narrators focalizing their sense impressions and cognition in various ways.

Therefore, focalization regulates the communicated, both in whole and in detail. From the broadest perspective, the limits of a mind's perceptions and cognitions also constitute a form of focalization: one can never communicate what is outside one's scope, so the presence of a certain virtual mind may result in the communicated being focalized in a way that would not be the case if another virtual mind, harboring other perceptions and cognitions, had been present. By the same token, actual minds can, naturally, only (try to) communicate what they have perceived and what they know or believe. From a narrower perspective, focalization is rather about choosing—for practical or more calculated reasons—to delimit the scope. As communicating minds may choose to pay attention to what they know about other minds, one of many ways of focalizing is to delimit one's scope to what one assumes to be the perceptions, knowledge, and ideas of other minds. Clearly, different minds within the same virtual sphere may focalize in ways that create tensions or even conflicts—clashes that may or may not be satisfactorily resolved by an overarching virtual narrator.

Overall, I believe that a clear notion of different levels of communicating, narrating, and focalizing minds is highly useful for understanding how communication at large and narration in particular is structured. It is essential that the conceptual framework is thoroughly transmedial, while at the same time pointing to the limits of transmediality. In the following chapter, where the attention will be on represented events, it should be borne in mind that events may appear both in narratives that actual or overarching virtual narrators are responsible for, and in narratives produced by embedded virtual narrators.

References

Alber, Jan. 2010. Hypothetical intentionalism: Cinematic narration reconsidered. In *Postclassical Narratology: Approaches and Analyses*, ed. Jan Alber and Monika Fludernik, 163–185. Columbus: Ohio State University Press.

Booth, Wayne C. 1961. *The Rhetoric of Fiction*. Chicago: University of Chicago Press.
Diehl, Nicholas. 2009. Imagining *de re* and the symmetry thesis of narration. *Journal of Aesthetics & Art Criticism* 67: 15–24.
Gaudreault, André. 2009 [1988]. *From Plato to Lumière: Narration and Monstration in Literature and Cinema*. Translated by Timothy Barnard. Toronto: University of Toronto Press.
Genette, Gérard. 1980 [1972]. *Narrative Discourse: An Essay in Method*. Translated by Jane E. Lewin. Ithaca, NY: Cornell University Press.
Hensher, Jonathan. 2016. Glimpsing the devil's tale? Towards a visual narratology of the fantastic in illustrated editions of Cazotte's *Le Diable amoureux*. *Journal for Eighteenth-Century Studies* 39: 663–681.
Jost, François. 2004. The look. From film to novel: An essay in comparative narratology. In *A Companion to Literature and Film*, ed. Robert Stam and Alessandra Raengo, trans. Robert Stam, 71–80. Malden, MA: Blackwell.
Mikkonen, Kai. 2011. Graphic narratives as a challenge to transmedial narratology: The question of focalization. *Amerikastudien/American Studies* 56: 637–652.
Mildorf, Jarmila, and Till Kinzel. 2016a. Audionarratology: Prolegomena to a research paradigm exploring sound and narrative. In *Audionarratology: Interfaces of Sound and Narrative*, ed. Jarmila Mildorf and Till Kinzel, 1–26. Berlin and Boston: de Gruyter.
Prince, Gerald. 1982. *Narratology: The Form and Functioning of Narrative*. Berlin: Mouton.
Thon, Jan-Noël. 2016. *Transmedial Narratology and Contemporary Media Culture*. Lincoln and London: University of Nebraska Press.

Open Access This chapter is licensed under the terms of the Creative Commons Attribution 4.0 International License (http://creativecommons.org/licenses/by/4.0/), which permits use, sharing, adaptation, distribution and reproduction in any medium or format, as long as you give appropriate credit to the original author(s) and the source, provide a link to the Creative Commons licence and indicate if changes were made.

The images or other third party material in this chapter are included in the chapter's Creative Commons licence, unless indicated otherwise in a credit line to the material. If material is not included in the chapter's Creative Commons licence and your intended use is not permitted by statutory regulation or exceeds the permitted use, you will need to obtain permission directly from the copyright holder.

CHAPTER 6

Events

Abstract This chapter scrutinizes the essential notion of represented events as a transmedial cornerstone of narration. Events should be understood as sudden or slow changes of conditions. Because events can be both concrete and abstract and generally very diverse, they can be represented by a broad range of media types far beyond the borders of verbal media. The distinction between actions and occurrences further helps to discern among different kinds of narratives: actions are events that result from acts of volition and occurrences are events that do not result from acts of volition. Finally, it is emphasized that some represented events are normally perceived to be more salient than others, which leads to hierarchization.

Keywords Transmedial narration • Existent • State • Event • Action • Occurrence

While the concepts of actual and virtual narrators and narratees are essential for understanding how narration is realized, narrating minds are not, as such, part of the narrative core—the investigation of which will start here. In this and the two subsequent chapters, I will examine the various constituents of this scaffolding core, the story, according to the definition of it as *represented events that are temporally interrelated in a meaningful way*. This chapter focuses on represented events.

The concept of event is potentially very complex. It has been investigated in great detail by David Herman (2002: 27–51), but for my purposes a comprehension that includes only the most essential features of the concept is needed. A general guiding principle to be observed is that it is not always possible to delimit the exact extension of events. Sometimes it may not be absolutely clear whether some represented happenings are best understood as one or several closely linked events (cf. Nanay 2009). Whereas this may be a philosophical difficulty, it does not constitute a problem for understanding how narration works.

STATES AND EVENTS

Nevertheless, the concept of event must be inspected and delineated sufficiently to operate transmedially. Chatman (1978) suggested that narratives include *existents* and *events*. Existents appear in represented space and events appear in represented time. Although this is a neat dichotomy that, at least partly, works well for its purpose of investigating narration in film and literature, it is too narrow for a more radical transmedial narratology. Confining existents to three-dimensional space means, in effect, that only materially existing objects and phenomena are captured. This largely excludes communication that is not primarily about what goes on in a physical place inhabited by concrete entities but is rather about more abstract notions. Although abstract thinking is also deeply colored by our experiences of existing in a three-dimensional, physical world, resulting in image schemas that bridge the mental and the material, there is a difference between thoughts and ideas that have a spatial character and physical objects and processes that are three-dimensional as such. Therefore, a truly transmedial narratology cannot delimit its scope to the representation of concrete existents but must include a comprehension of virtual spheres that contain representation of partly, mainly, or only abstract existents. This also means that the existents versus events dichotomy no longer builds on the clear-cut space-versus-time division.

Substantially modifying Chatman's dichotomy, I instead propose another initial distinction, namely between representing *what exists (existents)* and *how that evolves in time*. Existing entities may be material as well as mental and may be perceived as anything from concretely spatial to abstractly spatial or not spatial at all. Examples of existents would then include a cat represented by a still image, a balloon represented by moving images, the emotion of happiness represented by speech, the notion of high speed represented by a piece of writing, a toddler represented by gestures, and the idea of conflict represented by a meal. Represented existents like these are media characteristics that may be more or less transmedial: whereas the most abstract existents, such as conflicts, are likely to be most transmedial, the most concrete existents, such as balloons, are likely to be somewhat less transmedial. Media types based on developed systems of symbols, such as visual verbal language, have large representative scopes. As demonstrated in the previous sentences of this very text, several forms of both abstract and concrete existents can readily be represented by written words.

Media types based on visual or auditory iconicity may also represent a broad scope of existents. Not least, visual iconicity is a versatile representative tool: cats, balloons, and toddlers can be represented through straightforward similarity between representamen and object (meaning that, because of the resemblance, one directly conjures up inner images of cats, balloons, or toddlers). Adding an index makes it possible to also effortlessly represent existents such as happiness, speed, and conflict: visual icons of faces, airplanes, or cats can be formed in such ways that one does not only perceive a resemblance to these objects but also interpret them as really connected to more abstract existents. Represented faces that look happy also represent happiness, airplanes represented as flying also represent speed, and cats represented as fighting also represent conflict. Auditory icons, on the other hand, freely represent auditory objects that visual icons may represent only more indirectly: the mewing of a cat, for instance, can directly be represented by a sound resembling mewing, but only indirectly by a visual image of a cat with a certain facial expression. Thus, the transmediality of existents is not a question of either-or but rather of degrees between efficient and highly intersubjectively perceived transmediality and cumbersome and less intersubjectively perceived transmediality.

There is a wealth of represented existents. Investigating them all would amount to investigating the totality of communication, and investigating all their various transmedial potentials would be equal to investigating the entirety of transmediation.

How do existents evolve over time? Answering this question requires another distinction, namely between *states* and *events*. States are relatively stable conditions flanked by events, while events are sudden or slow changes of conditions. Thus, states tend toward lack of evolvement, whereas events comprise evolvement. Although there is clearly no definite way of saying when a slight modification of a state turns into a slow event, the distinction is operable and highlights important facets of what goes on both in the actual world and in virtual spheres.

Representing various kinds of existents is fundamental for all forms of communication and both states and events obviously presuppose existents; if there is no representation of anything that exists, there is clearly nothing that can evolve over time. One could say that representing states is the default position of communication. In a minimal act of communication, such as an actual communicator writing the word 'cat', the actual communicatee, if she understands English, will most probably form an interpretant based on the notion of an unchanging existent: a kind of animal with certain properties that does not evolve in time in any particular way. It is simply there; an existent in a certain state. Thus, representing events is optional in communication: 'the cat disappeared' involves an existent being connected to first a state and then an event: first the cat was simply there and then something happened—a sudden change of conditions leading to it no longer being there. Introducing such an event is the first step toward narration.

Just like existents, states and events can be material as well as mental; they may be directly perceived by the external senses as well as internally experienced. Whereas events such as balloons bursting or toddlers starting to cry are primarily perceived, events such as happiness being transformed to irritation or a conflict being resolved are often experienced.

Yet another distinction is needed to clarify the concept of event. As human beings, equipped with consciousness and advanced cognitive and emotive resources, most of us believe that there is a substantial difference between things that happen by themselves, because of physical forces freely operating in the universe, and things that happen because of cerebral processes. Again, we are faced with one of those difficult dichotomies that must certainly be thoroughly questioned and scrutinized but are nevertheless difficult to do away with. While it is easy to put theoretical pressure on the general material–mental dichotomy, and more specifically on the opposition between physical forces and cerebral processes—because cerebral processes actually adhere to physical forces—human interactions would be very difficult to handle if we did not recognize the vital difference between someone hitting someone else in the head and someone being hit in the head by a dead branch falling from a tree.

Consequently, in the context of human communication and transmedial narration it is useful to distinguish between two main forms of events:

actions and *occurrences*. Actions are events resulting from acts of volition, while occurrences are events not resulting from acts of volition (for a detailed discussion of the concept of action, see for instance Meister 2003). While this is not the forum to try to define the definite border between volition and non-volition, I leave the possibility open for understanding, for instance, certain acts performed by mentally severely ill living creatures as occurrences rather than actions. As other distinctions in this treatise, the distinction between actions and occurrences is not intended to cut reality into two pieces but rather to highlight important but debatable differences in order to get closer to a more complex understanding of the phenomena in question.

Examples of actions, either in our lived world or represented in various forms of communication, include a resting cat that decides to try to catch a mouse, a father who finds an empty balloon and blows it up, a lonely pensioner who buys a dog and becomes happy, a burglar who steels a car and drives away at high speed, a toddler jumping into a puddle, and a monkey who mocks another monkey and gets into conflict with it. Within literature and film narratology, represented concrete existents with conscious agency are often called *characters* (human beings, animals, or anthropomorphized objects).

Examples of occurrences, within or without communication, include a cat that falls ill because of eating an infected mouse, a balloon that gets lost because of strong wind, a happy pensioner who becomes sad because of the death of a friend, a speeding car that stops because there is no gas left, a toddler who gets soaked because of a sudden rain, and two monkeys who happen to find a delicious fruit simultaneously and start to quarrel. Like existents, events in the form of simple actions or occurrences are media characteristics that may be more or less transmedial. The most abstract events, such as conflicts that arise, are likely to be more transmedial, and the most concrete events, such as balloons blowing away, are likely to be less transmedial.

As narration is about representing events, all of these observations are relevant for analyzing how narratives can be formed; they are simply indispensable for studying the peculiarities of narration. Narratives must necessarily and self-evidently include represented existents. Whereas representing states—stable conditions of existents—is common and often sufficient in communication, narratives also comprise representations of changes in the conditions of existents: events. Narratives can also be constituted by represented events that are perceived as actions caused by volition, as occurrences not caused by volition, or as a mixture of the two. A miniature narrative such as 'Pearl Harbor was attacked by the Japanese air force, which brought the United States into World War II' is action-based. In contrast, the elementary narrative 'the Earth was hit by a giant meteor, which led to the extinction of dinosaurs' is occurrence-based. Confronted with a slightly more complex narrative such as 'because most people ignored the warnings of scientists, the accumulated emissions led to global climate changes; the consequences were massive involuntary migration and escalating worldwide famine and ethnic conflicts', one must conclude that it is based on a mixture of actions and occurrences. Naturally, occurrences can be represented so that they look like actions ('the eruption of the volcano was a warning to the people on the island who lived in sin but decided to repent') and actions may be brought forward as occurrences ('after having suffered such humiliation for many years, he was forced to kill her'). Media types based on symbol systems or visual iconicity are probably normally superior at expressing this kind of narrative subtlety.

HIERARCHIES OF EVENTS

The more events a narrative contains, the more interrelations will appear among events. Increased narrative complexity is likely to lead to stratification because, often, not all events are perceived to be equally important. Therefore, it is probably unavoidable to construe hierarchies of events; most perceivers of media products resulting in narrative virtual spheres of some complexity will find that events have partly different weight and function.

This was realized already in the infancy of narratology. Writing about 'motifs', which can approximately be understood as the smallest of events, Boris Tomashevsky suggested that "The motifs which cannot be omitted are *bound motifs*; those which may be omitted without disturbing the whole causal-chronological course of events are *free motifs*" (Tomashevsky 2012 [1925]: 68). In a similar vein, he proposed that "Motifs which change the situation are *dynamic motifs*; those which do not are *static*" (Tomashevsky 2012 [1925]: 70). Although there are only subtle differences between dynamic and bound motifs (if motifs change the situation, they cannot be omitted without altering the course of events) and between static and free motifs (if motives do not change the situation, they can be omitted without altering the course of events), the distinctions point to a substantial hierarchy of events in narratives. The difference between those represented events that are vital for the core of a narrative (what Tomashevsky called "the whole causal-chronological course of events") and those that are not highlights the fact that although the story, the scaffolding core of a narrative, consists of represented events that are temporally interrelated in a meaningful way, the whole narrative may contain less vital represented events that are not perceived to be part of the story.

Several decades later, Roland Barthes launched a similar distinction between more or less vital events. He stated that there are events that have "*cardinal functions*" and events that are merely "*catalysers*". For a function to be cardinal, he continued, "it is enough that the action to which it refers open (or continue, or close) an alternative that is of direct consequence for the subsequent development of the story. [...] Catalysers are only consecutive units, cardinal functions are both consecutive and consequential" (1977 [1966]: 93–94). Although Barthes was only writing about actions, the distinction may well be extended to also include occurrences.

Thus, represented events can to some extent, although hardly very exactly, be hierarchically ordered in concordance with Tomashevsky's and Barthes's ideas. Depending on the qualities of specific narratives, more or less clear-cut stratifications may be made in order to more clearly perceive meaningful relations among events. Although those two authors wrote mainly about literature, especially Tomashevsky's distinctions are formulated on a very general level and are truly transmedial. This means that they are important tools for analyzing transmediation of narratives: being able to identify events that are more vital than others means being able to more accurately find similarities among central structures shared by narratives realized by dissimilar media types.

However, the issue becomes more intricate when considering that narratives may embed narratives, which means that represented events are embedded in represented events (investigated by Genette 1980 [1972] and many others). As such, an embedded narrative may be considered to be an event in the overarching narrative that is or is not vital. Furthermore, events that are vital in an embedded narrative may or may not be considered vital in the overarching narrative. It is probably safe to say that it is rare that represented events can be straightforwardly stratified.

REFERENCES

Barthes, Roland. 1977 [1966]. Introduction to the structural analysis of narratives. In *Image—Music—Text*, trans. Stephen Heath, 79–124. New York: Hill and Wang.

Chatman, Seymour. 1978. *Story and Discourse: Narrative Structure in Fiction and Film*. Ithaca, NY and London: Cornell University Press.

Genette, Gérard. 1980 [1972]. *Narrative Discourse: An Essay in Method*. Translated by Jane E. Lewin. Ithaca, NY: Cornell University Press.

Herman, David. 2002. *Story Logic: Problems and Possibilities of Narrative*. Lincoln and London: University of Nebraska Press.

Meister, Jan Christoph. 2003. *Computing Action: A Narratological Approach*. Translated by Alastair Matthews. Berlin and New York: Walter de Gruyter.

Nanay, Bence. 2009. Narrative pictures. *Journal of Aesthetics & Art Criticism* 67: 119–129.

Tomashevsky, Boris. 2012 [1925]. Thematics. In *Russian Formalist Criticism: Four Essays*, trans. and ed. Lee T. Lemon and Marion J. Reis, 2nd ed., 61–95. Lincoln and London: University of Nebraska Press.

Open Access This chapter is licensed under the terms of the Creative Commons Attribution 4.0 International License (http://creativecommons.org/licenses/by/4.0/), which permits use, sharing, adaptation, distribution and reproduction in any medium or format, as long as you give appropriate credit to the original author(s) and the source, provide a link to the Creative Commons licence and indicate if changes were made.

The images or other third party material in this chapter are included in the chapter's Creative Commons licence, unless indicated otherwise in a credit line to the material. If material is not included in the chapter's Creative Commons licence and your intended use is not permitted by statutory regulation or exceeds the permitted use, you will need to obtain permission directly from the copyright holder.

CHAPTER 7

Temporal Interrelations

Abstract This chapter investigates temporal interrelations of represented events with an emphasis on dissimilarities among temporal interrelations. Two distinctions that are vital for grasping media differences are highlighted: possible temporal differences between (static or temporal) representing media products and (temporal) narratives, and potential temporal differences within narratives, more precisely between overall narratives and core stories. Particular attention is given to the convention of sequential decoding, which is important for inducing temporality in some forms of static media products. These explorations make it possible to understand both the transmedial possibilities and the media-specific restraints for narration.

Keywords Transmedial narration • Narrative time • Media product • Narrative: Story • Sequential decoding

Although the previous chapter was mainly attentive to the nature of represented events and their conceptual relations to existents and states, the last section also started investigating interrelations of events. This chapter will take the step toward examining *temporal* interrelations of events. In so doing, we move to the central part of the definition of story as represented events *that are temporally interrelated* in a meaningful way. As the notion of represented events being temporally interrelated is, as such, rather unproblematic—it simply means that events can be understood to precede and follow each other in various ways—the discussions will be concentrated on differences among temporal interrelations.

To be able to disentangle the crucial phenomenon of temporal differences in narration in a lucid way, I will repeat the three levels of narration that were first presented in Chap. 3:

- A media product with particular basic media traits and other formative qualities provides certain sensory configurations that are perceived by someone; these sensory configurations come to represent …
- … media characteristics forming a complete narrative with all its many specific details and features; furthermore, the perceiver comprehends that this narrative surrounds …
- … a scaffolding core, the story, consisting of represented events that are temporally interrelated in a meaningful way.

Inspecting this three-level distinction, one can discern two main ways in which narration can hold vital temporal differences: (1) There may be a difference between the basic temporal features of the media product and the narrative; (2) There may also be a difference situated within the narrative, namely between the complete narrative and the core of the narrative, the story.

These two kinds of temporal differences in narration—on one hand between the media product as representamen and the narrative as object and, on the other hand, within the object; that is, between the complete narrative and the scaffolding core story—are both central to understanding the possibilities, limitations, and particularities of transmedial narration.

Temporal Differences Between Media Products and Narratives

Investigating the first kind of temporal difference in narration, between the media product and the narrative, requires a methodical approach grounded especially in the spatiotemporal and semiotic modalities; although the material and sensorial media modes are not irrelevant, of course, there is no call to elaborate on them here beyond what was already done in Chap. 4.

In communication in general, there are four principal possibilities regarding temporal similarities and differences between a media product and a virtual sphere. There may be temporal media products representing temporal virtual spheres; temporal media products representing static virtual spheres; static media products representing temporal virtual spheres; and static media products representing static virtual spheres. As narratives are temporal virtual spheres, only two main options need to be considered: temporal media products representing temporal virtual spheres (narratives); and static media products representing temporal virtual spheres (narratives). Therefore, the simple initial observation to be made here is that, in principle, both temporal and static media products might represent temporal virtual spheres such as narratives. Moreover, it is fairly generally accepted that this is also the case in practice, as will be illuminated here in some detail.

A methodical overview of the abundance of intricate ways to narrate can begin with some comments on temporal media products forming narratives. In the simplest of cases, sensory configurations that are each understood to represent some event evolve one after another in the temporally unfolding media product. The default result of such an actual temporal sequence of representations, conditioned by the temporal progression of the media product, is that the temporal sequence of the media product corresponds to a temporal sequence in the virtual sphere. In these elementary cases, there is a strong parallelism between the temporal qualities of the media product and the narrative.

If one listened to the radio, for instance, and heard first a scream, then a bang, and finally the sound of something heavy falling to the ground, one would normally (unless other things speak against it) take those sounds to iconically represent a virtual sphere where something like this happens: first, someone sees a person with a gun and screams, then the gun is fired, and finally a body falls to the ground because it has been hit. The order of and the intervals between the sounds and the represented events would be understood to match each other (again as long as more complicated interpretations are not motivated). In instances like this, the narration is so straightforward that the distinctions between temporalities in media product, narrative, and story cannot be practically effectuated.

However, adding further details to the representation of these three events could lead to the construction of a more complex narrative. For instance, the actual narratee may perceive that in the virtual sphere there is a long temporal gap between the scream and the bang, or that the scream was in fact heard after the bang and the heavy fall. Temporal media types may indeed accomplish intricate narratives. The point is that temporal media products ultimately require very little, except their very temporality, to be capable of simple narration. The matching temporalities of temporal media products and temporal virtual spheres plainly facilitate narration.

The temporal difference between static media products and temporal virtual spheres requires more sophisticated conditions to make narration possible. I discern three main ways to bridge such a temporal difference and compensate for the lack of temporality in static media products. In practice, these conditions may be present separately or simultaneously.

The first prerequisite is a convention of sequential decoding. Such conventions, or strong habits, form the ground of a symbolic element also in those media types that are rather dominated by icons or indices. They can make static media products appear almost as if they were temporal, which means that their sequentiality may, by default, be understood to correspond to a temporal sequence in the virtual sphere. Some basic examples are regulated sequential decoding of iconic media types (such as series of still images), sequential decoding of iconic and indexical media types (like a succession of photographic still images), and sequential decoding of symbolic media types (with written verbal texts as the principal but not exclusive example). It is precisely the strong convention of sequential decoding that makes writing appear so similar to speech despite the fundamental difference between a static and a temporal media type.

The second prerequisite is the representation of temporal positions or relations. Icons may represent objects working as indices for temporal positions: clocks, the positions of the sun in the sky, objects connected to specific seasons of the year (snow, blossoming cherry trees, falling leaves, etc.), certain holidays, and so on. One example is visual two-dimensional still images that represent numerous hour-glasses indicating different time positions for several depicted events. Another example is tactile three-dimensional reliefs that iconically represent the growth of an infant through the development of bodily age characteristics connected to a number of crucial life events. Words or other symbols may represent temporal positions ('in the afternoon', 'Tuesday', '1984') or temporal relations ('earlier', 'first', 'now', 'then', 'later'). A visual, verbal, and two-dimensional text may represent a series of events temporally anchored to specific months of the year, or a tactile, verbal three-dimensional braille text may represent events that are bound together through different phases of the moon. All these devices may certainly occur also in temporal media types.

The third prerequisite is representation of objects that make it possible to create a temporal virtual sphere through inferences about past and future time. This is achievable because of collateral experience. As there are several forms of collateral experience, there are several means of achieving represented temporality through inferences about past and future time. Collateral experience in the form of general knowledge of both the natural and the cultural world often incites one to draw inferences of what has probably happened before and what will probably happen after a single event represented by a static media product. Any form of representation of, say, someone jumping from a bridge will normally lead to the perceiver inferring a temporal continuation: the person will fall down until something or someone rescues her or until she hits the ground or water underneath. This is what one's knowledge of the physical laws contributes. By the same token, the perceiver is likely to infer that something vital has anticipated the act of jumping: the single represented event cannot stand entirely alone, one presumes, for the simple reason that this is not how things work in the world that we are familiar with. So, the virtual sphere represented by the static media product may grow to include preceding events, such as the person having been forced by someone else to jump, having experienced a serious trauma that makes life unbearable, or having taken some heavy mind-altering drug. This is what one infers because of one's knowledge of human nature and culture.

As discussed above, general knowledge of the world may be developed to cognitive schemata, which means that inferences like these can be rather extensive. Any static media type representing an average person debarking a commercial airplane will open up for inclusion of a whole cognitive schema in the virtual sphere: the person has bought a ticket, then gone to the airport, passed security control, embarked, and spent some time sitting down in the aircraft before debarking, which will be followed—our cognitive schema tells us—by other standard procedures for airport arrival. In some cases, then, extensive cognitive schemata may provide static media products with the complete material for forming narratives.

Furthermore, collateral experience in the form of specific knowledge of already narrated stories may deliver additional events to the virtual spheres of static media products. If we are confronted with the representation of a little girl wearing a red hood and meeting a wolf in the woods, it may be almost unavoidable to see this event as part of a well-known story—given that the actual communicatee is familiar with the story, of course. The succession of events unfolds in the mind of the perceiver, creating a virtual sphere that is similar to those virtual spheres that have been formed in earlier perceptions of the story. Naturally, all forms of collateral experience are also relevant for temporal media types, although they are not always as urgent for achieving narration.

All these distinctions and elaborations not only contribute to our understanding of how static media types may narrate at all but also help us appreciate the balance between similarities and differences amid narration in temporal and static media types, respectively. They are, in brief, central for understanding the possibilities and limitations of transmedial narration.

Temporal Differences Between Narratives and Stories

We have seen that the temporality of the overarching narrative may be represented by either a temporal or a static media product. In the latter case, there is a temporal difference between the media product and the narrative; this is the first kind of temporal difference in narration. The second kind of possible temporal difference in narration is a difference situated within the narrative, namely between the temporality of the complete narrative and the temporality of the scaffolding core of the narrative, the story. It should be remembered, though, that it is not always possible to firmly establish the distinction between narrative and story in actual narratives, and that it only sometimes involves a temporal difference.

Why is it, then, that stories are sometimes construed in such a way that a temporal difference between the complete narrative, being more complex and elaborated, and the core story, consisting of the essence of temporal events in the narrative, is established? It is probably mainly because of an urge to think in terms of how the temporally interrelated events in the narrative would unfold if they would appear in directly perceived real life instead of being represented. Having a drive to understand what really happens around us is essential for our survival, and this includes a will to comprehend the ways in which events are interrelated.

In the case of temporal media types and static media types that are sequentially decoded because of conventions, the temporal qualities of the represented events in the overall narrative are, if not determined, at least strongly directed by the temporality or sequentiality of the media product. This is why the interrelations among events in the narrative may be deranged, so to speak, compared to how they would unfold if they were directly perceived in real life. Depending on what the actual narrator wants to emphasize, a story about someone who sees a person with a gun and screams, after which the gun is fired and a body falls to the ground, can be enwrapped in various forms of narratives emphasizing certain events rather than others, certain states rather than events, or certain interrelations among states and events. An efficient means of achieving such emphasis may be to manipulate the temporal interrelations of the story, thus forming narratives about, say, the state of the screaming person after the shot compared to the state before the shot, the dramatic event of the shooting, or the relation between the preceding state of the shooting person and the act of shooting. In general, an actual narrator may attract attention by starting with the most sensational event or create suspense by way of withholding it. She may also want to narrate a chain of events in the order she learnt about the separate events rather than in the order they possibly actually happened, thus emphasizing her own experience of putting the events together, which naturally creates a temporal difference between narrative and story.

In the case of media types not being temporal or sequentially decoded because of conventions, the order in which the represented events are encountered cannot, for obvious reasons, be determined by the (lack of) temporality and conventional sequentiality of the media product. This is not to say that the perceiver randomly explores the spatially represented events in the narrative. Some sensory configurations may be presented (through size or position, for instance) so that they are distinguished as more salient than others, which can lead to a rudimentary order of perception and partly decide the relative duration of certain perceptions. In museums, for instance, the visitor can even be directed by walls and other physical obstacles to follow a certain path and hence encounter represented events in an arranged order. Anyhow, the absent or relatively weak determination of how static but spatial media products are sensorially perceived in time weakens the possibility of construing a difference between the temporality of a narrative and the temporality of a core story. Perceivers of static media products that are not conventionally decoded sequentially presumably have little incentive to first construe an order of events in the narrative, with all its many specific details and features, and then discern another order of events in the core story; such a differentiation would be a detour for a perceiving mind striving to get a grip of what happens in the virtual sphere.

Thus, the exploration of temporal differences between narratives and stories is most, but certainly not exclusively, relevant for narration involving temporal media products and media products that are conventionally decoded sequentially. However, temporal differences between narratives and stories include more than differences of order and those other differences can be applied more broadly transmedially. Here I follow Gérard Genette, who has suggested three different sorts of temporal divergences in narratives regarding *order*, *duration*, and *frequency* (Genette 1980 [1972]: 33–160; the possible difference between the order of events in the 'plot' and the 'story' was already established in Tomashevsky 2012 [1925]: 67). Adopting and adapting this to a transmedial perspective, I suggest that there may be differences in the temporal order, duration, and frequency of represented events between the complete narrative and the core story. In other words, a difference may be perceived between how the order, duration, and frequency of events and states are represented in the narrative and how we assume that the order, duration, and frequency of events and states would appear in real life, not being represented. Therefore, construing a story may involve both a concentration and a rearrangement of represented events.

Let me briefly illustrate the idea of temporal differences with the aid of the example of listening to the radio and hearing first a scream, then a bang, and finally the sound of something heavy falling to the ground. As we have already noted, these sounds can be taken to represent the events of a narrative of someone seeing a person with a gun and screaming, after which the gun is fired and a body falls to the ground because it has been hit. Given the sparse sensory configurations transmitted by the radio, this is not the only possible narrative that may be construed. The point here is that if one reduces this narrative to a story, taking away a few marginal details, virtually the same order, duration, and frequency of events will remain.

However, such a correspondence is not necessarily the case in narration. Presume that one instead hears a bang, followed by a long pause. After that, an exceedingly, unnaturally long scream followed by a bang is heard and this sequence is repeated three times. Finally, after yet another long pause, the sound of something heavy falling to the ground is heard. Such an auditory, temporal, and iconic media product may well be understood as an artistic realization of the same simple story consisting of three interrelated events: a scream followed by a bang followed by a fall. In this case, however, there are substantial temporal differences between narrative (the temporal qualities of which are no doubt strongly directed by the temporal qualities of the media product) and story. The order differs because the narrative starts with the shot instead of the scream. The duration differs because the scream and the pause between bang and fall are longer in the narrative than in the story. The frequency differs because both the single scream and the single bang in the story are repeatedly represented in the narrative.

Narratology has long explored these forms of temporal differences, so it should suffice here to add that there may be temporal differences between overarching and embedded narratives and among separate embedded narratives that seem to have a common core and are possibly based on the same story. These narrative interrelations can no doubt be infinitely complicated.

The distinction between temporal qualities of the media product and the narrative, as well as the distinction between temporal qualities of the narrative and the story, are both central to understanding the possibilities and limitations of transmedial narration. Furthermore, the division between the two distinctions, which has a tendency to be blurred, allows for a more fine-grained understanding of temporal similarities and differences in narration. The distinction between temporal qualities of the media product and temporal qualities of the narrative is fundamental for exploring the basic narrative capacities of dissimilar media types. The distinction between temporal qualities of the narrative and temporal qualities of the story is widely recognized for highlighting vital narrative devices. However, this distinction has a limited transmedial reach: it is mainly applicable to temporal media types and media types that are conventionally decoded sequentially.

REFERENCES

Genette, Gérard. 1980 [1972]. *Narrative Discourse: An Essay in Method.* Translated by Jane E. Lewin. Ithaca, NY: Cornell University Press.

Tomashevsky, Boris. 2012 [1925]. Thematics. In *Russian Formalist Criticism: Four Essays*, trans. and ed. Lee T. Lemon and Marion J. Reis, 2nd ed., 61–95. Lincoln and London: University of Nebraska Press.

Open Access This chapter is licensed under the terms of the Creative Commons Attribution 4.0 International License (http://creativecommons.org/licenses/by/4.0/), which permits use, sharing, adaptation, distribution and reproduction in any medium or format, as long as you give appropriate credit to the original author(s) and the source, provide a link to the Creative Commons licence and indicate if changes were made.

The images or other third party material in this chapter are included in the chapter's Creative Commons licence, unless indicated otherwise in a credit line to the material. If material is not included in the chapter's Creative Commons licence and your intended use is not permitted by statutory regulation or exceeds the permitted use, you will need to obtain permission directly from the copyright holder.

CHAPTER 8

Internal Coherence

Abstract This chapter offers a semiotically colored model for interrogating meaningfully interrelated events in narratives. Based on our minds' inclination to perceive gestalts (i.e., intraconnected wholes), it is suggested that meaningful temporal interrelations among represented events be understood in terms of internal coherence. It is also put forward that the internal connections in narratives can be analyzed in terms of various sorts of contiguity, forming the basis for indices that bind together the numerous parts of narratives. Several theoretical perspectives and concepts, such as narrativization, are discussed. Finally, the results are demonstrated to be valid for the phenomenon of multimodal narration, which is central for understanding transmedial narration.

Keywords Transmedial narration • Coherence • Contiguity • Index • Narrativization • Multimodal narration

Whereas Chap. 7 scrutinized temporally interrelated events in general and differences among temporal interrelations in particular, this chapter will move on to the last part of the definition of story as represented events that are temporally interrelated *in a meaningful way*. Based on the inclination of our minds to perceive gestalts, intraconnected wholes, I suggest that meaningful temporal interrelations are understood in terms of *coherence*. Thus, narratives are virtual spheres that, to some extent, must be

© The Author(s) 2019
L. Elleström, *Transmedial Narration*,
https://doi.org/10.1007/978-3-030-01294-6_8

perceived as meaningful wholes; virtual spheres that, despite possible contrasts, tensions, ambiguities, uncertainties, and even incomprehensibilities, are ultimately internally coherent enough not to fall into separate pieces.

What does it mean to say that a virtual sphere is coherent? It may be, for instance, that represented persons and actions appear to be generally interrelated; events and moods seem to somehow follow from each other rather than occur randomly; details are apprehended as parts of discernible mental or material wholes; psychological states, ideas, and concepts are developed intelligibly; physical properties are associated to material items in a consistent way; physical and psychological actions lead to reactions that are linked to the actions; emotions can be understood in the context of other emotions and activities; concepts make sense considering the setting; or that entities and developments are felt to be proportional given the overall frame.

There are no clearly discernible borders between more and less coherent virtual spheres. Coherence is partly a quality of perception involving mental parameters that cannot be measured straightforwardly. By the same token, the difference between less coherent narratives and virtual spheres representing events that are unclearly interrelated is not always clear. There may be many cracks in a virtual sphere that is still kept together, but at some point it may be felt to break.

Kinds of Contiguity

Here, I will conceptualize coherence, or more precisely internal coherence of virtual spheres, in terms of indexicality. We have already established that indices stand for objects on the ground of contiguity, to be understood as real connections, and a main function of indices in communication is to form meaningful internal interrelations. Intracommunicational indexicality is semiosis creating bonds within a virtual sphere, connecting representamens on the ground of contiguity to objects that are drawn into or formed inside the virtual sphere as it evolves.

Apart from being able to hold represented space and time, a virtual sphere is spatiotemporal in the sense that it is formed by more or less continuous perception and interpretation of physically more or less demarcated media products. Even if the perception is interrupted (as when one stops reading a book and resumes the following day), or if parts of the media products are scattered (as when communication is spread to a combination of various media types that are accessible at different points of time and places), one has the mental capacity to (re)connect the pieces so that they form a consistent virtual sphere. Hence, the sensation of the constituents of the media product, as well as what they represent, is that they are minimally *co-present*. As perception and interpretation evolve they are often also understood to *interact*.

Narrative theory often emphasizes that events in narratives are related in terms of cause–effect, which can be understood as a strong form of interaction. While it may be mechanical causality or intentional causality, the latter kind is often privileged: narration is generally restricted to the representation of actions rather than occurrences.

However, some narratological research also comprises objections to an overly strict comprehension of interaction involving one event clearly causing another, suggesting more nuanced ways of understanding cause–effect as not necessarily very direct or absolute (see for instance Branigan 1992: 26–32). It can also be noted that the notion of cause–effect is not really used in physics, where one rather reasons in terms of connected conditions: given certain circumstances, certain things will happen because of the properties of involved objects and the physical laws. If one adds a mental side to this material conceptualization, one gets a tool for investigating interrelations among narrative events that is more subtle and multifaceted than the concept of cause and effect: given certain mental and material circumstances, certain things will happen because of the properties of involved material objects and the physical laws, and because of the individual features of involved minds and the psychological commonalities. In the context of narration, naturally, all these aspects are represented and part of virtual spheres.

Co-presence and interaction are two general forms of contiguity on a scale from weaker to stronger real connections among the constituents of virtual spheres. However, one may also think in terms of more specific subclasses of contiguity, understood as particular kinds of real connections that form the ground of indices. The following list of various kinds of relational channels between entities is in no way complete and there are no clear borders between the categories; the classification is merely intended to provide a broad overview of real connections by illuminating examples ranging from material to mental contiguity.

Contiguity that does not include mental activities in the relational channel between entities includes mechanical contiguity (e.g., between finger and fingerprint, or between a bow being drawn across strings and violin sounding); electromagnetic contiguity (such as between photons emitted from matter and digital photographs [see Godoy 2007], or between input in a computer and what is seen on the computer screen); chemical contiguity (between photons emitted from matter and classical photographs, or between added heat and boiling water); and organic contiguity (between disease and observable symptoms, or between a dead animal and a fossil).

Contiguity that includes corporeal and conscious or unconscious mental activities in the relational channel between entities includes, for instance, the combination of mental and mechanical contiguity (e.g., between the decision to use a pencil and written text, or between sudden rage and the smashing of a window) and the combination of mental and organic contiguity (such as between emotional state and voice quality, facial expression, and body posture; between refusal to eat and sensation of hunger).

Finally, there is contiguity that merely consists of conscious or unconscious mental activities in the relational channel between entities (between sensations and assumptions; between premises and conclusions). Thus, contiguity covers everything from concrete physical connections to abstract reasoning that often ultimately derives from experiences of corporeal relations.

These differentiations of forms of contiguity offer a refined way of understanding the many possible variations of meaningfully interrelated represented objects in virtual spheres in general and more specifically meaningfully interrelated events in narratives. The general and specific subclasses of contiguity illuminate the possible grounds of both intracommunicational indexicality (internal coherence of the virtual sphere) and extracommunicational indexicality (external truthfulness; to be discussed in Chap. 9). In the case of internal coherence, the contiguities are virtual. In the case of external truthfulness, even indices that build on stronger real connections (i.e., interaction) and reach out to the perceived actual sphere, represent only the world as one knows it. Not only mental, but also mechanical, electromagnetic, chemical, and organic contiguity are *presumed* contiguities formed by collateral experience. In the end, the extracommunicational and the intracommunicational domains are both mental.

NARRATIVIZATION

The concept of perceiving virtual spheres as consisting of meaningful relations among represented events—what I subsume here under the heading of intracommunicational coherence—has already been theorized in various ways. In the discussions of gestalt psychology in Chap. 2, I noted that our minds crave structure and sense. This might be reformulated in terms of contiguity: we crave real connections. As contiguities can be known to us only through mental operations, they must, I repeat, be conceptualized as *presumed* contiguities formed by collateral experience. This comports with ideas formulated within narratological research. Seymour Chatman noticed "our powerful tendency to connect the most divergent events" (1978: 47). By acknowledging this tendency, one is not far from embracing Monika Fludernik's concept of narrativization: "making something a narrative by the sheer act of imposing narrativity on it" (Fludernik 1996: 34). A relevant factor for such acts is *framing* (Wolf 2014, 2017), understood as all kinds of communicative elements that set the mind of the actual communicatee toward expecting narrativity and so increase the inclination to narrativize: to construe meaningful interrelations among represented events. Thus, narrativizing is not understood here as treating series of life events as narratives but as imposing narrativity on media products.

These ideas can fruitfully be compared with a classical psychological experiment by Fritz Heider and Marianne Simmel (1944) in which a large group of people were shown a short animated movie in which two triangles and a circle move around in relation to a rectangle with an opening. The figures and their movements were not randomly chosen. Nevertheless, the moving geometrical figures were automatically seen as representations of interacting animated beings and the rectangle as a house. A majority of the participants in the experiment interpreted the interactions as a connected story. A large but far from absolute consistency in these perceived stories was also reported. The researchers emphasized "the great importance which causal interpretation plays in the organization of the events into a story" (1944: 251).

Long before the heyday of narratology, this experiment demonstrated the power of narrativization and the transmedial nature of narration. Although not discussed or even mentioned, it also demonstrated that among the cognitive schemata used by the perceivers of the animated movie, one could not only find ideas about how animated beings such as humans interact in general, by nature, but also more specific cultural conceptions regarding gender behavior; in other words, stereotypes of how men and women are and how they act. Different narrativizations used partly different schemata originating in collateral experience of both nature and culture, resulting in partly different narratives.

A follow-up experiment by Bassili (1976) established that interaction among moving geometrical figures is perceived much more strongly during certain spatiotemporal conditions. Therefore, it is not the case that any kinds of stimuli are capable of triggering our inclination to perceive meaningful interrelations. Narrativization requires certain properties in the media products and we do not freely narrativize just anything to the same extent. Although human minds are inventive, crave meaningful coherence, and have the power to narrativize meager material, our minds additionally have constraints—there are limits to what one perceives to be meaningfully interrelated events (Bundgaard 2007). This leads to a certain degree of intersubjectivity among actual narratees. Consequently, whereas framing may sometimes be important for construing narratives, I would argue that it is neither a necessary nor a sufficient condition for narration. On one hand, media products may have qualities that make it practically unavoidable for most perceivers to interpret in terms of narration, independently of how they are framed. On the other hand, framing cannot incline us to narrativize any random sensory configurations.

Once again, one must conclude that understanding the emergence of narratives is a question of understanding both all kinds of surrounding factors of communication and the more inherent factors of different media products.

Multimodal Narration

Presumably, the results of the experiments by Heider and Simmel (1944) and Bassili (1976) can, in principle, be applied to all kinds of media. Narrativization does not occur only in the perception of solid, two-dimensional, temporal, visual, and iconic media products (cf. Neubauer 1997). It must also be expected that every change of mode of any of the media modalities may affect the way media products communicate. Another experiment, based on Heider and Simmel's animated movie, found that combining the movie with different kinds of music altered the total perceptions of narratives, to some extent (Marshall and Cohen 1988). This shows that, as most of us would probably expect, there is interaction among the various modes of media products in narration. During the last few decades, much empirical research has been dedicated to especially the interaction of sensory modes, such as vision and hearing, in communication in general.

Given that a majority of basic media types are multimodal—meaning that they have several material modes (like being partly organic, partly inorganic), several spatiotemporal modes (such as being both two-dimensionally spatial and temporal), several sensorial modes (being both visual and auditory, for instance), several semiotic modes (like being dominated by both iconic and symbolic signs), or several modes of more than one media modality—it is obvious that our minds have the capacity to bind these various modes together into one system of semiosis. For example, scientists know that sensory modes are connected and integrated in the brain, but know little about how this happens. Semiotic modeling, however, is more dependent on pragmatic observation than on detailed scientific evidence. Therefore, I claim that an important role of indices is to knit together the different modes of a media product so that an integrated virtual sphere, rather than a set of unrelated, mode-specific virtual spheres, can be created. Indices—representamens that call forth objects on the ground of contiguity—work effortlessly across modal borders simply because perceiving real connections among various modes is what our brains have been trained to do since the dawn of evolution. We know that solid, liquid, and gas-formed materiality interact; that our actual experience of space and time cannot be separated; and that our senses constantly cooperate to make sense of our surroundings.

On a deeper semiotic level, indices continue to connect all kinds of represented objects in a virtual sphere in order to achieve coherence. This is what I call intracommunicational indexicality: semiosis creating bonds within a virtual sphere. First, then, indices interconnect the actual perceptions of a possibly multimodal media product to prepare the formation of an integrated virtual sphere. At a later stage, indices interconnect the virtual constituents of the virtual sphere so that they can, if possible, form a coherent whole; the represented existents and events are perceived to interact. In the case of narration, indices form meaningful interrelation among virtual events in virtual time. This is the case whether the involved media products consist of a limited amount of material, spatiotemporal, sensorial, and semiotic modes (such as still images or written text) or are markedly multimodal (such as movies that are both spatial and temporal, visual and auditory, and iconic and symbolic).

References

Bassili, John N. 1976. Temporal and spatial contingencies in the perception of social events. *Journal of Personality and Social Psychology* 33: 680–685.

Branigan, Edward. 1992. *Narrative Comprehension and Film*. London and New York: Routledge.

Bundgaard, Peer F. 2007. The cognitive import of the narrative schema. *Semiotica* 165: 247–261.

Chatman, Seymour. 1978. *Story and Discourse: Narrative Structure in Fiction and Film*. Ithaca, NY and London: Cornell University Press.

Fludernik, Monika. 1996. *Towards a 'Natural' Narratology*. London and New York: Routledge.

Godoy, Hélio. 2007. Documentary realism, sampling theory and Peircean semiotics: Electronic audiovisual signs (analog or digital) as indexes of reality. *Doc On-line* 2: 107–117.

Heider, Fritz, and Marianne Simmel. 1944. An experimental study of apparent behavior. *The American Journal of Psychology* 57: 243–259.

Marshall, Sandra K., and Annabel J. Cohen. 1988. Effects of musical soundtracks on attitudes toward animated geometric figures. *Music Perception* 6: 95–112.

Neubauer, John. 1997. Tales of Hoffmann and others: On narrativizations of instrumental music. In *Interart Poetics: Essays on the Interrelations of the Arts and Media*, ed. Ulla-Britta Lagerroth, Hans Lund, and Erik Hedling, 117–136. Amsterdam and Atlanta, GA: Rodopi.

Wolf, Werner. 2014. Framings of narrative in literature and the pictorial arts. In *Storyworlds across Media: Toward a Media-Conscious Narratology*, ed. Marie-Laure Ryan and Jan-Noël Thon, 126–147. Lincoln and London: University of Nebraska Press.

———. 2017. Transmedial narratology: Theoretical foundations and some applications (fiction, single pictures, instrumental music). *Narrative* 25: 256–285.

Open Access This chapter is licensed under the terms of the Creative Commons Attribution 4.0 International License (http://creativecommons.org/licenses/by/4.0/), which permits use, sharing, adaptation, distribution and reproduction in any medium or format, as long as you give appropriate credit to the original author(s) and the source, provide a link to the Creative Commons licence and indicate if changes were made.

The images or other third party material in this chapter are included in the chapter's Creative Commons licence, unless indicated otherwise in a credit line to the material. If material is not included in the chapter's Creative Commons licence and your intended use is not permitted by statutory regulation or exceeds the permitted use, you will need to obtain permission directly from the copyright holder.

CHAPTER 9

External Truthfulness

Abstract This chapter proposes some analytical tools for understanding how communication in general and narration in particular can be truthful to what one perceives to be the actual world; how it can achieve external truthfulness. These external connections are scrutinized in terms of various sorts of contiguity, forming the basis for indices that connect narratives to the perceived actual world. The proposed analytical tools are intended to make it possible to understand the many ways in which the represented events in narratives can be connected to phenomena outside the narratives. The standard concept for theorizing this issue within narratology—fictionality—is critiqued and replaced with a multifaceted concept of (lacking) external truthfulness.

Keywords Transmedial narration • Truthfulness • Contiguity • Index
• Fiction • Fictionality

In Chap. 8, I circumscribed narration in terms of intracommunicational indexicality creating internal coherence. To conclude this second part of the treatise, I will also investigate narration in the light of extracommunicational indexicality forming external truthfulness. As internal coherence, external truthfulness is a concept that is potentially valid for all kinds of virtual spheres created in communication. Traditionally, however, and for good reasons, issues of truthfulness have often been connected to research on narration. When perceiving a narrative, nothing is more natural than to ask whether the story is 'true' or not; do the core events of the narrative correspond to events outside the narrative? The standard way of theorizing this issue within narratology is through the concept of fictionality. In this chapter, for reasons that will become clear, I will instead elaborate on the concept of extracommunicational indexicality.

Extracommunicational indexicality is semiosis that creates bonds between a virtual sphere and its surroundings, connecting representamens on the ground of contiguity to objects from outside the virtual sphere. I suggest this is external truthfulness in communication. Thus, the concept of *truthfulness* that I propose is to be understood as a conceived communicative trait; this is not to be confused with *truth*, which is understood as a feature of the actual, never fully accessible world. However, truth may possibly be approached through accumulated truthful communication and the observation of effects of further action on the basis of conceived truthfulness—if the effects of the actions correspond to what is predicted by the communication, there is a chance that truthfulness will come close to truth.

COMMUNICATORS AND NARRATORS

Approaching the issue of external truthfulness, one factor deserves special attention: communicating minds, understood as communicators (and more specifically narrators), not communicatees (narratees). As defined in this treatise, communication is about transferring cognitive import among minds. Therefore, the concept of communicator is germane. In related but clearly different ways, communicators are central to conceiving both the intracommunicational and the extracommunicational domain. To a certain extent, they are responsible for both internal (in)coherence and external (un)truthfulness. This comes about through representation. Communicators are made present to the mind of the perceiver, the actual communicatee, via representamens of the media products, and they may be objects in the virtual sphere itself, in other virtual spheres, or in the perceived actual sphere.

The starting point for this inquiry is the plain but fundamental observation that actual communicators, producing some cognitive import to be perceived by actual communicatees via media products, do not simply disappear behind the virtual spheres created in the perceivers' minds. In many situations, the actual communicator is decidedly represented by the media product and so becomes part of the virtual sphere. In an ordinary conversation, for instance, the word 'I' is often understood as an index, based on strong contiguity in tangible space and time, for the actual communicator using her body and its extensions as media products when uttering the word. To the extent that anything can be established at all, this is a determinable communicating mind that can even be engaged in two-way communication. In other situations, the actual communicator may be much more distant in both space and time and sometimes, such as when one looks at ancient rock-paintings, the actual communicator is not at all accessible and can only be construed as an idea of something that must have existed at some point. The painting becomes an index based on a weak contiguity that depends on the assumption that someone must have produced the visual configurations through actions of mind and hand. In any case, actual communicators are always, if they are parts of the perceived actual sphere, *perceived* actual producers' minds.

Represented actual communicators, originating in the perceived actual sphere, are objects that warrant external truthfulness, to varying degrees. Their existence in and collateral experiences of certain parts of the perceived actual sphere make it plausible that certain aspects of the communicated cognitive import are more or less truthful, even though, paradoxically, actual communicators in fact become virtual the moment they are represented. Of course, the representation of actual communicators is not in itself a guarantee of complete truthfulness (for instance, there are factors such as forgetfulness, misconceptions, and lies that disconnect parts of the intracommunicational domain from the extracommunicational domain), but the collateral experience of actual communicators makes it possible to partly decide upon the amount of contiguity that is present. This is a complex issue that cannot be developed further for the moment; here, I only want to stress that actual communicators are central extracommunicational objects; although their roles may vary considerably, they are always, at a minimum, necessary links to the perceived actual sphere.

Apart from representing actual communicators, media products may also represent overarching and embedded virtual communicators. Although emerging within the virtual sphere, overarching virtual communicators, like all intracommunicational objects, are ultimately construed by extracommunicational objects, which means that they may well be similar to actual communicators. In addition, media products may represent all kinds of communicators that have already been represented in other virtual spheres (one recognizes the communicators from earlier communication); these are extracommunicational objects that can be incorporated in a virtual sphere in intricate ways.

Kinds of Truthfulness

Although actual communicators are often central for the conception of external truthfulness through their presence in the perceived actual sphere, they do not, as such, determine the outcome of communication. Ultimately, it is the actual communicatees that perceive media products and form virtual spheres on the grounds of specific media traits and surrounding factors. More precisely, it is those media traits that are perceived to have real connections to the extracommunicational domain, and furthermore trigger indexical interpretation, that ultimately create external truthfulness.

One central question that has been largely missing in narratological research, and more broadly in communication research, is: To what exactly can communication, and therefore narration, be truthful? Only differentiating different kinds of external truthfulness can help us out of the trap of such unproductive dualities as truthful versus untruthful and fiction versus nonfiction, which too often lead to either-or ways of reasoning.

Therefore, I suggest that extracommunicational indexical objects—objects from the extracommunicational domain that are represented on the ground of real connections—can be classified variously, each category corresponding to a certain kind of truthfulness. Here, I will provide some prominent examples of such kinds of objects and truthfulness. It is not a rigid classification but rather an incomplete inventory of types that sometimes overlap, sometimes complement each other, and sometimes are in conflict. I do not propose that they should be treated as categories for compartmentalization; rather, they are flexible groupings for methodical investigations of truthfulness in communication.

Following the division of the extracommunicational domain into two parts, we may state that a virtual sphere can be truthful to objects in the perceived actual sphere or to objects in other virtual spheres; to our notions of the surrounding world or to our acquaintance with earlier communication. In turn, earlier communication may be truthful to objects in the perceived actual sphere or to objects in other virtual spheres. The notion that there may be truthful representations of other virtual spheres that do not represent the perceived actual sphere has previously been discussed in terms of making truthful performances and statements about so-called fictional characters (Colapietro 2009: 117; Searle 1975: 329).

Another division that follows from our earlier discussions in this treatise is that a virtual sphere can be truthful to objects that are material or mental. This is a crucial and, in a way, self-evident, but often neglected observation. According to my view, a concept of truthfulness that includes only real connections to materially observable states is perhaps easier to manage, but of little use.

Connecting to an age-old distinction of Aristotle, we can also say that a virtual sphere can be truthful to objects that are (more or less) universal or those that are particular (Aristotle 1997 [c. 330 BCE]: 81; cf. Gale 1971: 335; Gallagher 2006: 341–343; Walton 1983: 80). Some variations of this distinction would be to say that a virtual sphere can be truthful to objects that are typical or atypical; permanent or temporary; and global or local. This could perhaps be understood as a sort of statistical view on truthfulness, related to the probability of repeated contiguity in various environments and circumstances; truthfulness as a function of certain ways of framing the extracommunicational domain.

In a related manner, a virtual sphere can be truthful to objects that are wholes or to objects that are details (cf. Pavel 1986: 17). Truthfulness in detail does not guarantee a truthful whole and a truthful whole may harbor non-truthful details. This is truthfulness understood as perception of gestalts; truthfulness emanating from (in)attention to (absence of) singular real connections when construing the overall pattern of contiguity.

An important but more complex way of sorting extracommunicational indexical objects, partly coinciding with some of the earlier categories, is that a virtual sphere can be truthful to objects that have previously been manifested, that are currently manifested, that are bound to be manifested, or that may be manifested (cf. the concept of "possible worlds" in Pavel 1986: 46). One could perhaps even argue that a virtual sphere can be truthful to objects that should be manifested. These latter kinds of truthfulness rely heavily on mental contiguity.

In this context, it must also be noted that any material item can be drawn into the communicative act and become a media product working together with other media products or creating highly multimodal joint media products. In criminal trials, for instance, fingerprints and other pieces of evidence are framed so that they interact with standard basic media types such as speech, written text, still images, movies, and sound recordings that incorporate them to create a virtual sphere based on strong contiguity to the perceived actual sphere.

Summarizing these recent observations, and some earlier ones from Chap. 8, I suggest that all general varieties of contiguity (from weak co-presence to strong interaction), all kinds of indexical junctions (based on mechanical, electromagnetic, chemical, organic, and mental contiguity), and all types of indexical objects (in the perceived actual sphere or in other virtual spheres, material or mental, universal or particular, wholes or details, manifested previously, currently, or subsequently) are involved in claims to external truthfulness in communication. Consequently, they are all vital to external truthfulness in narration.

Truthfulness in So-Called Fiction

To close this chapter, and also Part II of the treatise, I will place external truthfulness in relation to the contrasting concepts of fiction and fictionality. Fictionality is normally understood as a supposed (at least partial) quality of certain qualified media types labeled fiction—"novel, short story, graphic novel, fiction film, television serial fiction, and so on" (Skov Nielsen et al. 2015: 62; cf. Searle 1975: 332)—and pertaining to representation of invented, unreal, and purely imaginary objects. Also, when fictionality is sometimes assumed to be a possible quality in nonfiction, it is circumscribed in terms of invention and unreality.

In other words, fictionality is supposedly not the representation of objects from the perceived actual sphere but solely of objects from the virtual sphere or other virtual spheres that do not involve the perceived actual sphere. This concept runs into trouble when one considers that all intracommunicational objects ultimately rely on extracommunicational objects, even though they emerge within the intracommunicational domain and may gain a sort of autonomy by being perceived as new gestalts. A minimal conclusion of this observation is that fictionality is very difficult to circumscribe because of the floating borders between extracommunicational objects and new intracommunicational gestalts. A more drastic conclusion is that there is no specific quality of fictionality, only sorts and degrees of truthfulness according to the categorizations in the last sections: degrees of contiguity from weak co-presence to strong interaction in various indexical junctions (based on mechanical, electromagnetic, chemical, organic, or mental contiguity) connecting to a variety of indexical objects (in the perceived actual sphere or in other virtual spheres, material or mental, universal or particular, wholes or details, manifested previously, currently, or subsequently). In less provocative terms, this would mean that the idea of fictionality is not necessarily meaningless or redundant but in dire need of a refined conception of the myriad ways in which communication can harbor low degrees of truthfulness.

If the term 'fictionality' is to be retained at all, it should not be understood as referring to distinct features but to a lack of certain sorts of truthfulness. In effect, this renders the term 'fictionality' superfluous. Hence, I argue that truthfulness and so-called fictionality are not two contrary qualities; rather, they represent different grades on the same scale—and one does not need two terms, and even less two concepts, to capture the variations of one phenomenon. I think it is more efficient to work with one homogeneous but indeed very complex concept of sorts and degrees of (lack of) truthfulness.

If the concept of fictionality is deserted or remodeled to a notion of lacking truthfulness, what is then left of fiction, which is supposedly based on fictionality? Under all circumstances, it is clear that one cannot make "a categorical distinction" between fiction and nonfiction (Yadav 2010: 191; cf. Ryan 1991). If the concept of nonfiction is to be retained in academic discourse, it must be understood as a range of qualified media types that are expected to have certain kinds of truthfulness. Fiction, an equally problematic concept, would then be a range of qualified media types that are expected to lack certain kinds of truthfulness. However, this does not eliminate the condition that there is truthfulness in both fiction (including qualified media types such as novels, animated cartoons, and ballads) and nonfiction (such as documentary films, scientific articles, and oral testimonies). This has been acknowledged in various ways by several scholars who otherwise differ in their conceptions and terminology (for instance, D'Alessandro 2016; Gale 1971; Grishakova 2008; Harshaw 1984; Ronen 1988; Ryan 1980; Searle 1975).

Because I find this conception of fiction versus nonfiction very coarse and unnecessarily cumbersome, I think it gives a better understanding of the varieties of truthfulness in communication if each qualified media type is investigated on a more fine-grained scale regarding expected truthfulness in terms of different kinds of contiguity and different kinds of extracommunicational indexical objects. I will illustrate this with some observations of a few qualified media types from the historical and cultural perspective in which the author of this treatise is situated.

Television news programs are normally expected to be strongly truthful in a variety of ways. They should preferably include photographs or film footage produced by electromagnetic or chemical contiguity. They should certainly be truthful to objects in the perceived actual sphere, but also to objects in other virtual spheres, meaning that earlier communication must be correctly reported. News programs should also have real connections to both material and mental objects; not only to persons, places, and events but also to objects such as ideas and emotions. Both wholes and details are expected to appear correctly. Importantly, these programs are expected to truthfully represent objects that are particular, regardless of their degree of universality, which means that atypical and temporary rather than permanent objects are also part of their norm. Furthermore, the programs should definitely be equally truthful to objects that have been manifested and those that are currently manifested—and, if possible, to objects that may or are bound to be manifested.

In contrast, historical paintings are expected to be strongly truthful in some ways and less truthful in others. To be counted as part of this qualified media type, a media product should be produced by mental and mechanical contiguity by a person possessing relevant collateral experience. A historical painting ought to be truthful to mainly material, visual objects. Although the quality of universality can certainly be included, it is primarily expected to have real connections to objects particular to a certain time and place. It is foreseen to be truthful to both wholes and details, although the very smallest details are often counted out. While the primary norm is to truthfully represent objects that have been manifested, this might well be combined with truthful representation of objects that may be manifested according to the idea that history can repeat itself.

A third example is science fiction novels that are expected to be more or less truthful in other ways compared to news reports and historical paintings. To a certain extent, they should be truthful to objects in other virtual spheres, meaning that their own objects should preferably correspond to other science fiction in order to make sense. Most readers probably anticipate such novels to represent more or less universal objects, and to discuss things in general and globally. Of course, this does not exclude truthful representations of atypical and spectacular objects. Naturally, science fiction novels are primarily expected to be truthful to objects that may be, and perhaps to some extent ought or ought not to be, manifested in the future.

My claim here is not that the sketched expectations of a handful of qualified media types are accurate, but rather that there are various and shifting anticipations of these kinds that are important for construing qualified media types. Media types and submedia, or genres, are often *qualified* (Elleström 2010) exactly regarding expected presence or absence of various sorts of truthfulness; qualified media types are partially defined by the very kinds of truthfulness in the media products that constitute them (cf. Wildekamp et al. 1980: 556). Thus, media type attributions such as 'this is a dinner conversation, but that is a legal testimony' can be understood as truth claims. Additionally, expected or even required varieties of external truthfulness and non-truthfulness are often envisaged to go hand-in-hand with certain styles and other media hallmarks that emphasize the media differences. In the end, however, qualified media types are certainly not stable entities but important pragmatic categories that vary through history, ideologies, and cultures. Mapping such manifold diversities is necessary in order to transcend the all too coarse fiction–nonfiction distinction.

In this concluding section of the last chapter of the second part of the treatise, I have already moved the discussion from basic to qualified media types. In the third and final part, the qualifying aspects of media types will be studied in some detail and from a decidedly narrative point of view.

REFERENCES

Aristotle. 1997 [c. 330 BCE]. *Aristotle's Poetics*, ed. John Baxter and Patrick Atherton. Translated by George Whalley. Montreal: McGill-Queen's University Press.

Colapietro, Vincent. 2009. Pointing things out: Exploring the indexical dimensions of literary texts. In *Redefining Literary Semiotics*, ed. Harri Veivo, Christina Ljungberg, and Jørgen Dines Johansen, 109–133. Newcastle upon Tyne: Cambridge Scholars Press.

D'Alessandro, William. 2016. Explicitism about truth in fiction. *British Journal of Aesthetics* 56: 53–65.

Elleström, Lars. 2010. The modalities of media: A model for understanding intermedial relations. In *Media Borders, Multimodality and Intermediality*, ed. Lars Elleström, 11–48. Basingstoke: Palgrave Macmillan.

Gale, Richard M. 1971. The fictive use of language. *Philosophy* 46: 324–340.

Gallagher, Catherine. 2006. The rise of fictionality. In *The Novel, Vol. 1: History, Geography, and Culture*, ed. Franco Moretti, 336–363. Princeton, NJ: Princeton University Press.

Grishakova, Marina. 2008. Literariness, fictionality, and the theory of possible worlds. In *Narrativity, Fictionality, and Literariness: The Narrative Turn and the Study of Literary Fiction*, ed. Lars-Åke Skalin, 57–76. Örebro: Örebro University Press.

Harshaw, Benjamin. 1984. Fictionality and fields of reference: Remarks on a theoretical framework. *Poetics Today* 5: 227–251.

Pavel, Thomas G. 1986. *Fictional Worlds*. Cambridge, MA: Harvard University Press.

Ronen, Ruth. 1988. Completing the incompleteness of fictional entities. *Poetics Today* 9: 497–514.

Ryan, Marie-Laure. 1980. Fiction, non-factuals, and the principle of minimal departure. *Poetics* 9: 403–422.

———. 1991. *Possible Worlds, Artificial Intelligence, and Narrative Theory*. Bloomington and Indianapolis: Indiana University Press.

Searle, John R. 1975. The logical status of fictional discourse. *New Literary History* 6: 319–332.

Skov Nielsen, Henrik, James Phelan, and Richard Walsh. 2015. Ten theses about fictionality. *Narrative* 23: 61–73.

Walton, Kendall L. 1983. Fiction, fiction-making, and styles of fictionality. *Philosophy and Literature* 7: 78–88.

Wildekamp, Ada, Ineke van Montfoort, and Willem van Ruiswijk. 1980. Fictionality and convention. *Poetics* 9: 547–567.

Yadav, Alok. 2010. Literature, fictiveness, and postcolonial criticism. *Novel* 43: 189–196.

Open Access This chapter is licensed under the terms of the Creative Commons Attribution 4.0 International License (http://creativecommons.org/licenses/by/4.0/), which permits use, sharing, adaptation, distribution and reproduction in any medium or format, as long as you give appropriate credit to the original author(s) and the source, provide a link to the Creative Commons licence and indicate if changes were made.

The images or other third party material in this chapter are included in the chapter's Creative Commons licence, unless indicated otherwise in a credit line to the material. If material is not included in the chapter's Creative Commons licence and your intended use is not permitted by statutory regulation or exceeds the permitted use, you will need to obtain permission directly from the copyright holder.

PART III

Demonstrating the Principles

It is now time to fully engage in the issue of narration in qualified media types: media types that are formed not only by basic modality modes but also by the origin, delimitation, and use of media in specific historical, cultural, and social circumstances, and furthermore by their communicative and perhaps aesthetic traits; what they can do for certain people in certain environments (Elleström 2010: 24–27). Part III exemplifies narration in diverse qualified media types: painting, instrumental music, mathematical equations, and guided tours. These qualified media types are grounded on partly very dissimilar basic media types, which also makes it possible to highlight the fundamental importance of media modalities for narration. The four brief investigations will additionally illustrate how historically and socially qualified media types establish, in different ways, conventions that facilitate narration. Through habits and experiences we form expectations and learn how to interpret certain features of qualified media types as narrative supports. Each investigation will pay attention to the core elements of narratives, *represented events that are temporally interrelated in a meaningful way*, entrenched in the other general communicative fundamentals that have been elaborated throughout the first two parts of the treatise.

Reference

Elleström, Lars. 2010. The modalities of media: A model for understanding intermedial relations. In *Media Borders, Multimodality and Intermediality*, ed. Lars Elleström, 11–48. Basingstoke: Palgrave Macmillan.

CHAPTER 10

Narration in Qualified Media Types

Abstract This chapter illuminates and roughly summarizes some vital concepts and ideas of the whole treatise. Narration in four diverse qualified media types is explored: painting, instrumental music, mathematical equations, and guided tours. These qualified media types are grounded on partly very dissimilar basic media types, which also makes it possible to highlight the fundamental importance of media modalities for narration. The four investigations also illustrate how historically and socially qualified media types establish conventions that facilitate narration. Overall, the four investigations elucidate the usefulness of the theoretical framework developed in the treatise and highlight the media similarities and differences that make narration a profoundly transmedial but media-dependent phenomenon.

Keywords Transmedial narration • Qualified media • Painting • Instrumental music • Mathematical equations • Guided tours

In selecting qualified media types I have avoided those that have been most popular in narratological research, such as various forms of literature, film, and comics. To push the transmedial perspective, I chose to inspect media types that challenge overly narrow limits of narration. I begin with two already partly explored artistic qualified media types—painting and instrumental music—and end with two unexplored 'non-artistic' qualified media types: mathematical equations and guided tours. As my goal is to highlight the broad transmedial applicability of essential narrative concepts, the four investigations will be structured similarly, while also revealing in some detail the media-specific differences.

Painting

There is a long history of research on the issue of narration in painting. Because painting is normally understood as a qualified form of the basic media type of still image, the results of this research can, to some extent, be extended to narration in still images in general. Paintings are still images in that they are usually expected to be solid (and generally inorganic), two-dimensionally spatial and non-temporal, visual, and predominantly iconic. Being predominantly iconic means that the visual surface is at an initial stage primarily understood to resemble the objects that they represent, although the represented objects are not necessarily concrete and visual. Paintings, like other forms of media products, may be cross-modally iconic, meaning that the iconicity is based on similarities among, for instance, different sense perceptions, and between concrete and abstract entities (Elleström 2017). This means that so-called abstract or non-figurative art may also be iconic, representing objects such as rhythms and patterns of sound or tactile sensations, or more abstract notions such as clashes, speed, harmony, chaos, or rest.

Although the capacity to hold cross-modal iconicity facilitates transmediation among different media types in general, and also transmediation of narratives, narration in painting faces one obstacle: because the materiality of still images does not evolve in time, painting is a static media type. As already noted, this puts narration to the test because non-temporal media products do not readily represent temporal relationships among events. However, as I concluded earlier, this does not eliminate the narrative capacity of still images and hence paintings.

This is not the forum for extensive elaborations on how painting as a qualified media type can be delineated. One crucial point of the concept of qualified medium is that qualified media types are bound to vary and change, which means that I can only make approximations here. If one initially circumscribes paintings as still images that are handcrafted by people using various techniques for applying color to a surface, one may note that there is a multitude of specific traditions and functions of paintings in various cultures. Of course, no one really knows precisely how ancient people used and appreciated for instance rock-paintings, and still today paintings have rather different functions depending on culture and other contexts. Paintings may be expected to have, say, religious, aesthetic, educational, or practical uses, or a mixture of them all. For more thorough investigations, therefore, it is probably more useful to think in terms of several interrelated rather than one single qualified medium of painting.

As painting is such a broad media category, there are virtually no limits to the kinds of events that a painting may depict. Anything that can be represented by visual still images may be harbored within painting conceived as an all-embracing qualified medium. Naturally, criteria for what kinds of events qualify for proper painting vary considerably depending on time and culture. For instance, at a certain moment in a certain place, only events from Christian history and mythology might be accepted. Additionally, there are genres of painting that further qualify what kinds of existents, states, and events should be included. Therefore, genres may appropriately be called submedia.

Some paintings, such as so-called still lifes, represent only states, such as food lying on a table. Although it is not impossible to narrativize such states, there is a huge difference between still lifes and paintings depicting myriad people eating, fighting, or playing. In the latter case, both concrete events such as jumping and falling and abstract events such as winning and losing may be directly represented. Given a sufficient amount of events, they may also be hierarchized by the actual communicatee on the basis of the appearance of the media product—the painting. On one hand, represented events may be given a dominant role because of, say, large size, foreground location, or central position on the two-dimensional surface of the painting. On the other hand, represented events may be perceived to be principal because of their existential weight; someone dying in the background may well be a more essential event than someone having a beer in the foreground.

Given the capacity of paintings to represent a multitude of concrete and abstract events, both actions and occurrences, it is fair to say that paintings, photographs, and other still images have "narrative implications" (Kafalenos 1996). It is also clear that painting and other qualified media types based on visual still images have, for thousands of years, developed conventions that enhance narration. In semiotic terms, this adds a symbolic element to the predominantly iconic medium of painting. Research in the historical development of ancient qualified media types such as epic literature, vase painting, and illustrated written religious texts have discerned three methods of realizing already known literary narratives in visual art (Wickhoff 1895: 8–9; Weitzmann 1947: 12–33). These categories are echoed in later and more general research on transmedial narration (such as Kibédi Varga 1988; Wolf 2003: 189–191). Formulated in my own terminology and with the addition of some reflections, narration is achieved through the three following means:

- One single confined two-dimensional space in which one event is directly represented. This event calls other temporally interrelated events to mind so that they can together form a narrative. As stated in Chap. 7, there are at least two ways of achieving narration in this way. Either collateral experience in the form of general knowledge of the natural and cultural world is called forth to provide additional events, or collateral experience in the form of specific knowledge of an already existing narrative complements the directly represented event so that other temporally interrelated events can be added.
- One single confined two-dimensional space in which several events are directly represented. These events can be sorted temporally by the perceiver and form a narrative. As there are conventions for this kind of interpretation in painting, beholders are invited to construe such temporal interrelations.
- Several confined two-dimensional spaces in which one event per space is directly represented. These spaces are supposed to be perceived sequentially. In other words, narration is enhanced through a convention of sequential decoding in analogy with the convention of reading written verbal texts.

In principle, one could add a fourth possibility (Kibédi Varga 1988); namely, several confined two-dimensional spaces in which several events per space are directly represented. These spaces should also be perceived sequentially.

There are clearly many ways of representing several temporally interrelated events in painting and these may include temporal differences between narratives and stories (Genette 1980 [1972]: 33–160). A conventionally decoded sequence of events may form a narrative in which the order of events differs from the order in the story. Also, paintings that are not sequentially arranged can hold a temporal difference between narrative and story in terms of frequency: a single confined two-dimensional space in which several events are represented may represent what is perceived to be the same event several times (meaning at different places), although it only happens once in the story.

Thus, narration in painting profits from habitually grounded ways of ordering represented events or even perceiving them in a certain order. In addition, painting often includes another symbolic element: visual verbal titles. These may clearly add to the overall narration by representing interrelated events that, for instance, specify or augment the events represented by the visual icons. Werner Wolf emphasized the importance of captions pointing to "cultural scripts" and thus enhancing narration (Wolf 2003: 191).

Given that there are several interrelated media types of painting, rather than one single type, the issue of expected truthfulness in painting is anything but straightforward. However, it is important to emphasize that even though painting is generally categorized among other art forms as some sort of 'fiction', successful painting is certainly not believed to lack truthfulness. Although indexicality in painting can clearly be understood in terms of texture and patterns of color having real connections to how the artist's tools mechanically formed the surface—which is relevant when establishing who actually created a painting—mental contiguity is of more immediate interest for most perceivers of painting. In terms of mental contiguity, the way in which things have actually been experienced by minds exposes other forms of truthfulness to the many kinds of mental and material objects in the perceived actual sphere. Obviously, different types of painting are expected to represent different forms of indexical objects understood in terms of, say, universals or particulars and wholes or details. Whereas paintings of the crucifixion of Christ should be truthful to how humans generally suffer or exult, paintings of specific historical events are supposed to be truthful to the appearance of individuals. Whereas impressionistic works are expected to be truthful to how the whole visual area is perceived, so-called *trompe l'oeil* paintings must be truthful to both the whole and all of its details. All these forms of truthfulness may be part of painted narratives.

Instrumental Music

Narratological research, including studies in transmedial narration, often ignores the rather extensive research in musical narration. Márta Grabócz (2008) provides an overview of the many ideas about narration in music and the subject is somewhat controversial. Malgorzata Pawlowska (2014) offers a good summary of the shifting opinions on the existence of narration in music. The hesitation to embrace the idea of music being potentially narrative does not so much concern music including song, or having words integrated in other ways, as music (almost) completely lacking verbal components—which I refer to here as instrumental music. As the concept of narration is still strongly associated with verbal media types, some scholars consider music that has perhaps at most an abstract title as the only verbal constituent to be non-narrative, almost by definition. I will refrain from explicitly arguing against these views, which are often variously formulated in nuanced ways, and instead pick up some rewarding suggestions of how to conceptualize narration in music. My contention is that it is both unproblematic and constructive to consider some instrumental music narrative.

The presemiotic basic media traits of music are fairly clear-cut. Materially, music simply consists of vibrating air. These vibrations are temporal because they change as time passes; all music is perceived within a certain time frame. Music may also be three-dimensionally spatial to a certain extent. If the point of departure for the vibrations is one single location, like a guitar, the vibrations are spread in the room in a fairly symmetrical way, making us perceive the music as one sensation, albeit distributed in space. If the points of departure for the vibrations are several locations—such as a guitar, a flute, and a set of drums—the vibrations are spread throughout the room so that one may discern spatial differences. This three-dimensionality of music is more diffuse than the three-dimensionality of, say, a gesturing body, but concrete enough to contribute to the signification of music. Although music may be defined to include the visual perception of for instance performing musicians, I delimit it here to the auditory.

It is perhaps more controversial to state that the dominant semiotic mode of instrumental music is iconicity. It would require a large detour from the primary objective of this treatise to explain the many conflicting ideas about musical signification, or more generally musical meaning. Therefore, here I only suggest that musical signs are auditory signs largely referring to motions, emotions, bodily experiences, and cognitive structures on the ground of similarity. Melodies, pitches, intervals, rhythms, dynamics, sound qualities, and the way they together form ever-developing structures represent similar structures in the externally perceived common world around us, in the internally perceived personal world within us, and in the emotionally and cognitively experienced mental domain within us.

Representing emotions, for instance, is not the same as evoking emotions: a listener can perceive that a piece of music represents happiness without becoming happy herself.

From a presemiotic point of view, instrumental music is no doubt suitable for representing temporality and therefore potentially for narrating because all musical media products evolve in time. The challenge of narration in instrumental music concerns the semiotic rather than the spatiotemporal modality, mainly because of the absence of well-developed symbolicity in the form of verbal language.

Instrumental music, understood as a qualified medium and not just any form of communicative non-verbal sound, is generally expected to have some sort of aesthetic qualities, in a broad sense (including lighter as well as more highbrowed aesthetics). Because instrumental music, just like painting, is such a broad category, a more detailed study would have to make distinctions among an abundance of all forms of submedia, genres, in order to give a representative picture. Like all qualified media types, instrumental music is qualified differently in different periods, cultures, and subcultures. Since virtually all research on narration in music that I am aware of concerns Western classical (tonal) music, this will also be my point of departure—not because I think it is necessarily the best illustration of narration in instrumental music but because it makes it easier to incorporate existing research in my argumentation.

Having swiftly established that the representation of temporality poses no problem for instrumental music, the remaining core question for narration concerns the representation of events. It is evident that instrumental music does not freely represent events that are as clearly and intersubjectively definable as many events represented by language-based media types using advanced symbol systems, media types using visual icons (photography, dance), or both (television news, comics). In those media types, events can often also be connected to concrete existents, which make them more palpable. In instrumental music, events must primarily be understood in terms of changes in tempo, dynamics, sound qualities, keys, and so forth. Events such as these, and also the existents that they are grounded on, are abstract rather than concrete. Nevertheless, existents and events represented by auditory icons can certainly be perceived as having meaningful interrelationships.

Anthony Newcomb discussed this in terms of temporally ordered musical events where the listener experiences directedness, continuation, and potential (Newcomb 1987). Also, Eero Tarasti treated narration in music in terms of temporally emerging tensions and forces among events; he additionally reasoned more specifically, in terms of musical entities such as "actants" or "actors" that fulfill different functions in the musical narrative (Tarasti 1994). Susan McClary emphasized relations among themes and keys and the possibility of thinking about tunes as "protagonists", together forming tensions in the temporal development and possibly disruptions of expectations (McClary 1994, 1997; cf. Seaton 2005). Broadening the scope, Vera Micznik wrote about musical narration in a more far-reaching sense, beyond directions, forces, and tensions among abstract events represented iconically (Micznik 2001). She also considered connotations (which I would translate as indexicality) and sense created by musical conventions (which I would call symbolicity). Although limited in their scope compared to those extensive systems of symbols that we call verbal languages, such musical symbols also connect more directly to the exterior and can hence represent more concrete existents and events such as happenings in a pastoral scene. Thus, musical narration including symbols is closer to narration in verbal media types than to musical narration primarily based on icons.

Convention-based semiosis in instrumental music can be grounded not only on habits of representing certain existents and events but also on more specifically narrative conventions: habits of composing music that facilitate narration. Newcomb (1987) developed a rather general analogy between narration in written literature and instrumental music in terms of rule-governed, temporal perception of sensations representing events supported by narrative conventions that lead to certain expectations of what will follow, although these may or may not be fulfilled.

The above-mentioned researchers variously thought of represented events as actions or occurrences. Including notions such as actants and protagonists means that music is understood to represent conscious entities, minds, which act and thus create events in the form of actions. Consequently, it is possible but not necessary to think about musical events in terms of actions; also without represented minds that act there may be events in the form of occurrences. It must also be added that although the prerequisite for narration consists of representation of temporally interrelated events, the sometimes accented three-dimensionality of musical sounds also facilitate distinct spatial divisions of represented events: listening to musical sounds coming from different directions may trigger the creation of a virtual sphere containing spatially separated events. It is additionally clear that musically represented actions and occurrences, distributed in time and possibly also in space, are generally more or less hierarchized by listeners: all changes of conditions are not considered to be equally important.

It goes without saying that collateral experience of the perceiver in the form of cognitive schemes and knowledge of earlier narratives may be vital for the realization of narration in instrumental music. This means that very simple verbal titles can also make event-structures of known narratives or cognitive schemes present to the mind of the perceiver; these event-structures may then be realized or reinforced by the unfolding musical structure. Noting this, we are already on our way to explain narration in so-called program music, which includes more comprehensive verbal elements and hence falls beyond the borders of instrumental music as defined here.

Anyhow, perceiving music with or without verbal components involves striving toward grasping some sort of internal coherence. If one is aware of a title pointing toward something more concrete, one normally tries to incorporate this in the virtual sphere. If the piece of music only has an abstract title referring to musical form (like 'Piano Concerto No. 2') or no title at all, it may nevertheless not be self-evident how the parts belong together; it might be necessary to construe an overarching virtual narrator being responsible for, say, the representation of harsh clashes between existents and events that are best understood as ironic. Robert Hatten argued that narration in music includes some extreme contrasts in instrumental music that may be understood as shifts in the "level of discourse"; a sudden change in mood may place "all of the previous musical discourse in a new perspective" (Hatten 1991: 88). Avoiding the notion of discourse, I understand this as musical pieces presenting embedded virtual narrators introducing new and contrasting events or focalizing already represented events in a completely different way. Such ruptures may or may not be successfully reconciled by an overarching virtual narrator.

Narration in instrumental music can also be complex in other ways. There may be temporal differences between the complete narrative and the scaffolding core story, more specifically differences between the order, duration, and frequency of states and events in the narrative and the story (Genette 1980 [1972]: 33–160). This was investigated by Fred Everett Maus (1991) in reference to musical analyses made by other musicologists. Exemplifying differences in duration, Maus noted that a "musical tragedy" may be understood to have a story that lasts for months or years, while its complete narrative only lasts for eight minutes (Maus 1991: 31).

Differences in order are illustrated with a 'cadential gesture', normally heard toward the end of a piece, instead being displayed early; one may then perceive a temporal disjunction between the temporal development of the story (which is concluded by the cadence) and the temporal development of the narrative (which presents the cadence at the outset) (Maus 1991: 28–30). Such a cadential gesture may actually be heard several times in the same piece, which may then be understood as appearing only once in the story but several times in the complete narrative; this would constitute a difference in frequency (Maus 1991: 30).

Musical narration, like all other forms of narration, may be perceived to be more or less truthful, and instrumental music is also qualified as a type of medium on the basis of, among other things, expected truthfulness. Again, it is important to note that instrumental music must be understood in terms of a variety of submedia (such as Indian instrumental ragas, progressive rock without song, or string quartets), so it is impossible to deliver anything but very general remarks here. Anyhow, it makes little sense to me to understand instrumental music (just as other forms of communication) in terms of fictionality. Although it cannot have the same kind of contiguity and refer to the same kind of indexical objects as certain other media types, it is very much connected to the perceived actual sphere. I suggest thinking in terms of mental contiguity, how things have actually been experienced by minds. Instrumental music is often expected to be, and indeed frequently is, truthful to objects such as motions, bodily experiences, emotions, and cognitive structures in general. Indexical objects like these are known to us not least through personal (external or internal) experiences and perceptions of both material and mental phenomena, so representations of them can be perceived to be more or less truthful. Because of our deeply shared resources of feeling and thinking, the indexical objects of music are often perceived to be highly universal.

Mathematical Equations

Compared to painting and instrumental music, mathematical equations constitute a quite different qualified media type that has hardly been researched in terms of narration. Nevertheless, it is a media type that illuminates the concept of narration in several ways. Although mathematicians may find some equations elegant, to some degree, they are not considered an art form, and compared to most other forms of communication it is rather abstract; nevertheless, I believe its narrative capacity is striking.

Apart from figures representing numbers, mathematics is full of symbols that are rarely or never used outside this specific communicative domain. The basic feature of equations is that they state that two things are equal, which is symbolized by an equals sign (=). Moreover, equations include variables, also called unknowns, that are often represented by letters such as x, y, and z. The point of equations is to communicate a mathematical problem that can be solved through calculation so that the two so-called expressions on each side of the equals sign can be demonstrated to be equivalent. This includes determining the values of the variables. The solution of the simple equation $2 + x = 5$ is that the variable x stands for 3 because 2 + 3 equals 5.

Investigating the media modalities of mathematical equations makes it clear that the basic modes of equations are virtually identical to those of written verbal language. Hence, mathematical equations and written verbal language overlap smoothly in various ways and they can both efficiently be transmediated to spoken verbal language; that is, they can be read. Although both these qualified media types can, in principle, be realized in rather varied material and spatiotemporal settings, they normally appear on solid, inorganic, static, and two-dimensional surfaces. They are visual and their most salient signs are symbols: letters in the case of most Western languages, and, in the case of mathematics, figures and a range of specifically mathematical symbols (although there are also figures in language and letters in mathematics). Semiotically, however, written verbal language as well as mathematical equations may also be considerably iconic and hence semiotically multimodal. The equals sign in itself consists of two identical lines representing the absolute similarity of the two expressions in equations. The other mathematical symbols are placed on the surface in such a way that one may perceive similarities in gaps, distances, internal relationships, proportions, and other spatial qualities. The equivalence of the two expressions is represented iconically through their mirrored positions to the left and to the right, respectively, of the equals sign. Hence, the two expressions can be seen as signs for each other, so to speak.

We have noted that equations—like paintings, but unlike instrumental music—are non-temporal, which means that they do not absolutely effortlessly represent temporally ordered events. Unless one knows what an equation is and how to proceed in interpreting it, little significance will come out of it—and certainly not a virtual sphere containing temporally interrelated events. Furthermore, mathematical equations have evolved as media products in different cultures for thousands of years; therefore, as with other qualified media types, there is a historical dimension to consider. Like painting and instrumental music, equations do not constitute one single variation but rather a plenitude of submedia with intricate specific traits and widely different levels of complexity. Nevertheless, they are all expected to hold the specific communicative core quality of being tools for solving mathematical problems that may be more or less connected to understanding properties of the world.

Equations can represent existents that are not only numeral abstractions. Albert Einstein's famous formula $e = mc^2$ represents the interrelations among energy, mass, and the speed of light. However, these interrelations involve certain calculable relationships. Thus, equations in physics, chemistry, and engineering freely mix representations of existents that are anchored in the physical qualities of the world and mathematical existents such as numbers and proportions. Therefore, represented events in mathematical equations may be changes of conditions involving both more concrete and more abstract states.

A simple equation such as $1 + 1 + 4 - 5 = x$ represents events understood as changes of numeral and proportional states. It can be read verbally as 'one plus one plus four minus five equals ex'. Whether the equation is read verbally or not does not affect its potential status as a narrative; either way, it represents a series of numeral changes—a succession of interrelated events. Nevertheless, a transmediation to a more elaborate verbal narrative might make the narrative core of the equation more visible: 'I was alone in the kitchen when my wife came home. Soon after that, also our four children arrived, but after a while I saw five family members go out in the garden. As I was very tired it was all very confusing: how many were actually left in the kitchen?'

One of the differences between the mathematical equation and its verbal transmediation, apart from the very concise narrative (consisting of virtually only a minimal core story) being expanded to a somewhat more elaborate narrative, is that events in the form of occurrences are changed into actions. Events represented by equations, if the latter are not embedded in other forms of communication, are normally occurrences rather than actions. Some events in equations have a larger impact (adding four rather than one is a more significant change of states), which means that they in a way can be hierarchized. In another way, however, all events are equally vital, as ignoring even the tiniest of them will invalidate any equation.

Mathematical narration in equations, involving represented events that are temporally interrelated in a meaningful way, is very much supported by conventions that facilitate narration. One such principal qualifying convention is, of course, the rule of sequential decoding. Like Western written verbal language, one must decode equations (roughly) from left to right and from top to bottom, in order to get the events in the right order (the represented events must be understood to follow the order of decoding the mathematical signs). There are many other conventions that I will not go into great detail with here. For instance, the use of parentheses determines how events are to be separated from each other and ordered. A section of an equation such as $3y + 7$ is totally different from $3(y + 7)$. $3y + 7$ means that first the variable y is tripled, and then seven is added to the product. On the other hand, $3(y + 7)$ means that seven is added to the variable y, and then this sum is tripled. Because of the parenthesis convention, the two sections represent different events that are ordered in different ways and are therefore parts of different narratives. It can be concluded that represented events in equations are not only interrelated in general but temporally interrelated in specific ways.

Clearly, just as paintings or pieces of instrumental music, not all equations are best understood as narratives. A formula such as $e = mc^2$ is hardly a narrative. An equation such as $3x + 2^2 + 6 - 4 = 3 \times 4 + 3$, on the other hand, represents several interrelated events that change the developing numeral state: numbers are multiplied, squared, added, and subtracted. These calculations cannot easily be performed without collateral experience of numeral changes in one's life environment and, especially in the case of more complicated equations, mathematical training increasing one's ability to keep track of a multitude of intricately interrelated events. The assumption in every equation, including those that cannot be seen as narratives, is that they hold total internal coherence. Only when the balance between the two expressions is perfect, meaning that they represent exactly the same numeral state, can the equation be considered correctly formed or solved. Solving an equation involves strong mental indexicality: semiosis based on contiguity or real connections. This means that there are simply no options regarding how to connect the signs of the media product to what we think of as the mathematical reality. Signs such as 2^2 are symbols, of course, but also indices to the extent that they put us in direct relation with general principles (in this case, a perceived actual existence of the quality of twoness and the operation of multiplying a number with itself).

I also think that it is fruitful to make a distinction between narratives and stories in equations, at least to a certain extent. We have already stated that it is essential to decode the mathematical symbols in a specific order and that this order largely determines the order of represented events in the narrative. However, an important incentive for construing stories out of more extensive narratives is, we have also noted, to understand how the temporally interrelated events in the narrative would unfold if they would appear in directly perceived real life instead of being represented, and evoking such an incentive for equations seems almost nonsensical (unless, of course, they are embedded in other forms of communication representing more concrete aspects of the experienced world). This means that, normally, it would probably make little sense to think in terms of temporal differences (regarding order, duration, and frequency) between narrative and story in mathematical equations.

However, this does not eliminate the usefulness of the distinction between a complete narrative and a scaffolding core story, at least in equations that can be simplified. Isolating variables and simplifying equations are established ways of solving them step by step. For instance, $3x + 2^2 + 6 - 4 = 3 \times 4 + 3$ can initially be simplified so that $3x + 4 + 6 - 4 = 12 + 3$ remains. Simplifying it even further may lead to $3x + 10 - 4 = 15$. Perhaps this stage of the simplification could be considered the core story of the complete narrative. Further simplification leads to $3x + 6 = 15$, then $3x = 9$, and finally $x = 3$, which is the solution—the final state after the events have passed by, so to speak.

However, I doubt the usefulness of the concepts of embedded virtual narrators and narratees for equations. The virtual spheres of mathematical equations are strictly regulated and can hardly allow for alternative perspectives. Furthermore, the focalization of the actual or overarching virtual narrator must be very strong to fulfill the firm requirements of equations. The expected truthfulness of the qualified medium of mathematical equations, as its internal coherence, is based on mental contiguity leading to indexical junctions: the logics of mathematics is not only valid within the virtual spheres of equations but also reflects conditions in the perceived actual sphere, including what we understand to be physical laws. Thus, the indexical objects in the perceived actual sphere may be both mental and material. As equations can be applied to both general phenomena and particular circumstances, the indexical objects in the perceived actual sphere may additionally be universal as well as particular, and wholes as well as details.

Guided Tours

The last qualified media type to be investigated is guided tours, which, to the best of my knowledge, have not yet been researched in terms of narration. This is a form of communication that may rely on a wealth of modes; hence, it exemplifies multimodal narration at its extreme. As a guided tour goes on, all forms of media products can be incorporated in a composite media product that integrates an increased amount of more or less dissimilar media types—together forming an amalgamated media type with its own character. Virtually all modes of the material, spatiotemporal, sensorial, and semiotic modalities may be included in guided tours, which entails that narration, and communication in general, can be realized through many different resources interacting in a multitude of complex ways that can only be hinted at here. In order to make the presentation somewhat more focused, I will mainly discuss one of many variations of guided tours: guided city tours.

All guided tours are temporal; they are not only perceived in time, which is the case for all media products, but, like music, they are unfolded in time. This is a convenient media trait for narration as it makes it possible to represent events in a certain order that cannot be escaped. However, guided tours can include parts that are static rather than temporal, although introduced in a temporal flow. As a guided city tour goes on, sculptures, reliefs, paintings, and other forms of visual, static, and two-dimensional images are likely to appear. Also, various forms of inscriptions, signposts, and other static, visual, and verbal media products that must be sequentially decoded in order to make full meaning can be expected to be integrated. It is clear that these static incorporated media products may represent events that contribute to an overall narrative.

I would argue that guided tours are generally expected to be narrative. In other words: narration is one of the qualifying traits of guided tours. Most people who embark on a guided tour do not simply want to learn about a row of isolated states and events but also about their meaningful temporal interrelations. Spatial movement is another qualifying trait of guided tours. The participants in a guided city tour expect to be involved not only in a temporally evolving media product but also in a three-dimensional, spatially evolving media product; they expect to walk or be driven around in the city—otherwise, it is simply not a tour. Furthermore, a tour cannot be considered a guided tour if it does not include a guide. Thus, a classic guided tour includes one or several corporeally present persons acting as guides, meaning that they are the actual narrators being present together with the participants, the actual narratees. Variations of guided tours, such as those involving audio guides (pre-recorded voices) instead of living persons, are not considered here.

As guided tours are composite media products potentially incorporating virtually all kinds of media products, they can represent practically all kinds of states and events, whether these events are actions or occurrences. These many forms of events may clearly be more or less strongly interrelated. It may be presumed that the actual narratees of guided city tours normally form a hierarchy of essential historical events, with certain major events at the top forming a scaffolding story: when the city was founded, when it became a capital, when it was invaded, when the most famous buildings were erected, when major parts of it were destroyed in a fire, and so on, and how these events are interrelated.

Given the open structure of guided tours, which normally include a broad variety of media products, probably often representing a multitude of also only vaguely interrelated events, actual narratees are likely to construe partly rather different hierarchies of events. Naturally, all forms of background knowledge of history, culture, geography, and so forth—and of earlier narratives including events related to these areas—facilitate the creation of relevant interconnections among the many directly represented events, as well as events that are not directly represented by the guided tour. Because most people expect guided tours to be narrative (they are often conventionally understood to constitute narratives), they are probably narrativized to a high degree in accordance with cognitive schemes related to historical, cultural, and political development.

However, diverging background knowledge among actual narratees may contribute to the formation of both differing stories and dissimilar hierarchies of events. Another factor that may add to a disintegration of stories construed by different perceivers is the complexity of representations in guided tours, meaning that there are no definite borders between a guided tour and everything surrounding it; almost any observation of the actual narratees may be incorporated into what they perceive to be the guided tour. In order to make sense of the sometimes scattered or even conflicting mass of represented events, either clearly within or in the border zone of the guided tour, the perceivers are likely to construe an overarching virtual narrator that, to some extent, reconciles uncertainties and conflicts and pushes the many represented states and events toward internal coherence.

Probably much more often than not, guided tours harbor temporal differences between narrative and story (Genette 1980 [1972]: 33–160). It is difficult to arrange a guided city tour in such a way that the temporal order of the represented events in the complete narrative correspond precisely to the temporal order in the story. Moving through a city involves encountering quarters, buildings, squares, and monuments related to historical events that do not follow the path of the tour. Thus, the guide must, at least to some extent, jump back and forth among the historical events and still explain their interrelations so that a scaffolding story can be captured. Using spoken language, this is easily achieved though phrasings such as 'this happened long before …' or 'this would lead to the events that I described earlier …'. Differences in duration are also unavoidable. As a guided city tour only lasts for a few hours and the history of a city can be counted in decades, centuries, or even millennia, the duration of the narrative, directed by the actual duration of the media product, is very much shorter than the duration of the story—the duration of states and events as we assume they have appeared in real life. Differences in frequency are also ordinary elements in guided city tours. For instance, the most central events in the story, such as a collective action like a revolution or a natural occurrence like an earthquake, are likely to be represented several times in the narrative even though they occur only once in the story; this is modeled on our assumptions of real life events. In an abundantly multimodal media type such as guided tours, these repeated representations of the same events can be realized in a multitude of ways: through speech and gestures, sculptures, monuments, inscriptions, leaflets, engravings, paintings, ruins, or walls with cracks caused by the earthquake or bullet holes from the revolution.

It may not be self-evident how to understand the status of narrators in relation to the many media products that are integrated in a guided tour. However, it is clear that a guide is an actual narrator being present at the tour, using her own body and its extensions as media products while talking, gesticulating, and pointing, and also drawing objects in the surrounding into the realm of communication so that they act as media products. This presence enables two-way communication between the actual narrators and the actual narratees—the tour participants. There may also be communication among the actual narratees that adds to the guided tour.

All this gives the participants the potential double role of actual communicators, possibly narrators, and actual narratees (in other words: they can interact with the guided tour). On top of this, the participants of a guided tour encounter various media products produced by other, often absent, actual narrators. Thus, one can say that a guided tour involves not only the actual narrators constituted by the present guides (and possibly the participants) but also a variety of mainly absent, living or dead actual narrators.

However, one could also argue that although the many media products in a guided tour are certainly directly perceived by the actual narratees, they are actually embedded in the overall narrative produced by the guides. Disregarding those many media products that are unavoidably haphazardly perceived by the participants, beyond the control of the guide, the media products that the guide actually incorporates in the tour (in a planned or improvised way) are not only perceived by the participants but in effect represented by the guide when somehow communicatively drawing the participants' attention to them. There is no conflict between something being simultaneously perceived and represented: the guide might say 'there you can see the castle' and at the same time point to it while the perceiver simultaneously actually looks at the castle, representing a certain event in political history. This means that while the architects, builders, and those who ordered the building of the castle are the initial actual communicators of, say, political power or cultural belonging, both these actual communicators and the media product—the castle—become embedded in the guided tour when represented by the guide. I believe that this view is feasible. Therefore, it is reasonable to say that whereas there are only a few present actual narrators of guided tours (the guides and possibly some participants), there are a multitude of embedded virtual narrators of embedded represented media products. In the end, it is the focalization of the actual narrators—what they know and what they choose to highlight about the city—that primarily determines how the narrative is formed.

Finally, it should be noted that the qualified medium of guided tours tangibly illuminates the relevance of truthfulness for narration. As many of the locations of the represented events in guided city tours are not only represented but also actually perceived during the tour, the door is open for media products to have direct and strong interactional contiguity with the represented states and events in the narrative. There is an important difference between someone saying that a certain city has a castle bearing material witness to both an earthquake and a revolution, and someone saying that the castle in front of you has traces of these dramatic events. Directly perceiving a building with cracks and holes, which could have resulted from an earthquake and battles, may add a vital indexical dimension: the participants of the guided tour directly perceive material objects that are drawn into the communication and thus acquire the function of media products; media products that are really connected to the perceived actual sphere.

Therefore, in contrast to the previously discussed qualified media types, guided city tours provide opportunities for not only mental but also material contiguity between representamens of the media product and objects in the perceived actual sphere. While in the case of cracks and bullet holes the perceived contiguity is mechanical, also electromagnetic, chemical, organic, and other forms of material contiguity may be involved in achieving external truthfulness in guided tours. Grossly simplifying the issue of indexical object in guided tours, it can be surmised that participants of city tours expect them to be truthful to both material and mental objects, to both details and wholes, to objects that are manifested previously and currently rather than subsequently (to history rather than future), and to particulars rather than universals (to one specific city rather than all cities). Additionally, it is generally both accepted and perhaps even expected that guided city tours are truthful to other virtual spheres; that is, to earlier communication regarding the city in question, including accepted history writing but also legends, fanciful tales, and other submedia types that are less directly anchored in the perceived actual sphere.

Rounding Off

I will stop here before my account of transmedial narration becomes too repetitive. More and lengthier examples of qualified media types would no doubt highlight additional media-specific intricacies, but I doubt that the essential transmedial principles would be further clarified. However, the conceptual tools that I have offered in this treatise for understanding and analyzing narration should be useful for disentangling the narrative potential of any form of communication. They should also, hopefully, be helpful for perceiving both media similarities and media differences that facilitate or obstruct transmediation of narratives among different forms of basic and qualified media types.

References

Elleström, Lars. 2017. Bridging the gap between image and metaphor through cross-modal iconicity: An interdisciplinary model. *Iconicity in Language and Literature* 15: 167–190.
Genette, Gérard. 1980 [1972]. *Narrative Discourse: An Essay in Method*. Translated by Jane E. Lewin. Ithaca, NY: Cornell University Press.
Grabócz, Márta. 2008. Classical narratology and narrative analysis in music. In *A Sounding of Signs: Modalities and Moments in Music, Culture, and Philosophy*, ed. Robert S. Hatten, Pirjo Kukkonen, Richard Littlefield, Harri Veivo, and Irma Vierimaa, 19–42. Imatra: International Semiotics Institute.
Hatten, Robert. 1991. On narrativity in music: Expressive genres and levels of discourse in Beethoven. *Indiana Theory Review* 12: 75–98.
Kafalenos, Emma. 1996. Implications of narrative in painting and photography. *New Novel Review* 3: 53–64.
Kibédi Varga, A. 1988. Stories told by pictures. *Style* 22: 194–208.
Maus, Fred Everett. 1991. Music as narrative. *Indiana Theory Review* 12: 1–34.
McClary, Susan. 1994. Narratives of bourgeois subjectivity in Mozart's *Prague Symphonie*. In *Understanding Narrative*, ed. James Phelan and Peter J. Rabinowitz, 65–98. Columbus: Ohio State University Press.
———. 1997. The impromptu that trod on a loaf: Or how music tells stories. *Narrative* 5: 20–35.
Micznik, Vera. 2001. Music and narrative revisited: Degrees of narrativity in Beethoven and Mahler. *Journal of the Royal Musical Association* 126: 193–249.
Newcomb, Anthony. 1987. Schumann and late eighteenth-century narrative strategies. *19th-Century Music* 11: 164–174.
Pawlowska, Malgorzata. 2014. Musical narratology: An outline. In *Beyond Classical Narration: Transmedial and Unnatural Challenges*, ed. Jan Alber and Per Krogh Hansen, 197–220. Berlin and Boston: De Gruyter.
Seaton, Douglas. 2005. Narrative in music: The case of Beethoven's 'Tempest' sonata. In *Narratology Beyond Literary Criticism: Mediality, Disciplinarity*, ed. Jan Christoph Meister, Tom Kindt, and Wilhelm Schernus, 65–81. Berlin and New York: Walter De Gruyter.
Tarasti, Eero. 1994. *A Theory of Musical Semiotics*. Bloomington: Indiana University Press.
Weitzmann, Kurt. 1947. *Illustrations in Roll and Codex: A Study of the Origin and Method of Text Illustration*. Princeton, NJ: Princeton University Press.
Wickhoff, Franz. 1895. Der Stil der Genesisbilder und die Geschichte seiner Entwicklung. In *Die Wiener Genesis*, ed. Wilhelm Ritter von Härtel and Franz Wickhoff, vol. 2, 1–96. Vienna: F. Tempsky.
Wolf, Werner. 2003. Narrative and narrativity: A narratological reconceptualization and its applicability to the visual arts. *Word & Image* 19: 180–197.

Open Access This chapter is licensed under the terms of the Creative Commons Attribution 4.0 International License (http://creativecommons.org/licenses/by/4.0/), which permits use, sharing, adaptation, distribution and reproduction in any medium or format, as long as you give appropriate credit to the original author(s) and the source, provide a link to the Creative Commons licence and indicate if changes were made.

The images or other third party material in this chapter are included in the chapter's Creative Commons licence, unless indicated otherwise in a credit line to the material. If material is not included in the chapter's Creative Commons licence and your intended use is not permitted by statutory regulation or exceeds the permitted use, you will need to obtain permission directly from the copyright holder.

REFERENCES

Abbate, Carolyn. 1991. *Unsung Voices: Opera and Musical Narrative in the Nineteenth Century*. Princeton, NJ: Princeton University Press.
Abbott, Lawrence L. 1986. Comic art: Characteristics and potentialities of a narrative medium. *Journal of Popular Culture* 19: 155–176.
Alber, Jan. 2010. Hypothetical intentionalism: Cinematic narration reconsidered. In *Postclassical Narratology: Approaches and Analyses*, ed. Jan Alber and Monika Fludernik, 163–185. Columbus: Ohio State University Press.
Almén, Byron. 2008. *A Theory of Musical Narrative*. Bloomington and Indianapolis: Indiana University Press.
Alpers, Svetlana. 1976. Describe or narrate? A problem in realistic representation. *New Literary History* 8: 15–41.
Altman, Rick. 2008. *A Theory of Narrative*. New York: Columbia University Press.
Aristotle. 1997 [c. 330 BCE]. *Aristotle's Poetics*, ed. John Baxter and Patrick Atherton. Translated by George Whalley. Montreal: McGill-Queen's University Press.
Arvidson, Mats. 2016. *An Imaginary Musical Road Movie: Transmedial Semiotic Structures in Brad Mehldau's Concept Album 'Highway Rider'*. Lund: Lund Studies in Arts and Cultural Sciences.
Bal, Mieke. 2009. *Narratology: Introduction to the Theory of Narrative*. 3rd ed. Toronto: University of Toronto Press.
Barthes, Roland. 1977 [1966]. Introduction to the structural analysis of narratives. In *Image—Music—Text*, trans. Stephen Heath, 79–124. New York: Hill and Wang.
Bassili, John N. 1976. Temporal and spatial contingencies in the perception of social events. *Journal of Personality and Social Psychology* 33: 680–685.

Bergman, Mats. 2009. Experience, purpose, and the value of vagueness: On C. S. Peirce's contribution to the philosophy of communication. *Communication Theory* 19: 248–277.

Berning, Nora. 2014. Narrative journalism from a transdisciplinary perspective: A narratological analysis of award-winning literary reportages. In *Beyond Classical Narration: Transmedial and Unnatural Challenges*, ed. Jan Alber and Per Krogh Hansen, 117–135. Berlin and Boston: De Gruyter.

Booth, Wayne C. 1961. *The Rhetoric of Fiction*. Chicago: University of Chicago Press.

Bordwell, David. 1985. *Narration in the Fiction Film*. London and New York: Routledge.

Branigan, Edward. 1992. *Narrative Comprehension and Film*. London and New York: Routledge.

Bremond, Claude. 1964. Le message narratif. *Communications* 4: 4–32.

Brewer, William F. 1987. Schemas versus mental models in human memory. In *Modelling Cognition*, ed. Peter Morris, 187–197. Oxford: Oxford University Press.

Brilliant, Richard. 1984. *Visual Narratives: Storytelling in Etruscan and Roman Art*. Ithaca, NY: Cornell University Press.

Brooks, Peter, and Paul Gewirtz, eds. 1998. *Law's Stories: Narrative and Rhetoric in the Law*. New Haven, CT and London: Yale University Press.

Bundgaard, Peer F. 2007. The cognitive import of the narrative schema. *Semiotica* 165: 247–261.

Campbell, Richard, and Jimmie L. Reeves. 1989. TV news narration and common sense: Updating the Soviet threat. *Journal of Film and Video* 41: 58–74.

Canary, Robert H., and Henry Kozicki, eds. 1978. *The Writing of History: Literary Form and Historical Understanding*. Madison: University of Wisconsin Press.

Chatman, Seymour. 1978. *Story and Discourse: Narrative Structure in Fiction and Film*. Ithaca, NY and London: Cornell University Press.

Cohn, Dorrit. 1990. Signposts of fictionality: A narratological perspective. *Poetics Today* 11: 775–804.

Colapietro, Vincent. 2009. Pointing things out: Exploring the indexical dimensions of literary texts. In *Redefining Literary Semiotics*, ed. Harri Veivo, Christina Ljungberg, and Jørgen Dines Johansen, 109–133. Newcastle upon Tyne: Cambridge Scholars Press.

D'Alessandro, William. 2016. Explicitism about truth in fiction. *British Journal of Aesthetics* 56: 53–65.

de Freitas, Elizabeth. 2012. The diagram as story: Unfolding the event-structure of the mathematical diagram. *For the Learning of Mathematics* 32: 27–33.

Diehl, Nicholas. 2009. Imagining *de re* and the symmetry thesis of narration. *Journal of Aesthetics & Art Criticism* 67: 15–24.

Doxiadis, Apostolos. 2012. A streetcar named (among other things) proof: From storytelling to geometry, via poetry and rhetoric. In *Circles Disturbed: The*

Interplay of Mathematics and Narrative, ed. Apostolos Doxiadis and Barry Mazur, 281–388. Princeton, NJ and Oxford: Princeton University Press.

Eakin, John Paul. 2008. *Living Autobiographically: How We Create Identity in Narrative*. Ithaca, NY: Cornell University Press.

Elleström, Lars. 2010. The modalities of media: A model for understanding intermedial relations. In *Media Borders, Multimodality and Intermediality*, ed. Lars Elleström, 11–48. Basingstoke: Palgrave Macmillan.

———. 2014a. *Media Transformation: The Transfer of Media Characteristics Among Media*. Basingstoke: Palgrave Macmillan.

———. 2014b. Material and mental representation: Peirce adapted to the study of media and arts. *The American Journal of Semiotics* 30: 83–138.

———. 2017. Bridging the gap between image and metaphor through cross-modal iconicity: An interdisciplinary model. *Iconicity in Language and Literature* 15: 167–190.

———. 2018a. Modelling human communication: Mediality and semiotics. In *Meanings & Co.: The Interdisciplinarity of Communication, Semiotics and Multimodality*, ed. Alin Olteanu, Andrew Stables, and Dumitru Bortun, 7–32. Cham: Springer.

———. 2018b. A medium-centered model of communication. *Semiotica* 224: 269–293.

———. Forthcoming. Coherence and truthfulness in communication: Intracommunicational and extracommunicational indexicality. *Semiotica*.

Fludernik, Monika. 1996. *Towards a 'Natural' Narratology*. London and New York: Routledge.

Foster, Susan Leigh. 1996. *Choreography and Narrative: Ballet's Staging of Story and Desire*. Bloomington: Indiana University Press.

Gale, Richard M. 1971. The fictive use of language. *Philosophy* 46: 324–340.

Gallagher, Catherine. 2006. The rise of fictionality. In *The Novel, Vol. 1: History, Geography, and Culture*, ed. Franco Moretti, 336–363. Princeton, NJ: Princeton University Press.

Gaudreault, André. 2009 [1988]. *From Plato to Lumière: Narration and Monstration in Literature and Cinema*. Translated by Timothy Barnard. Toronto: University of Toronto Press.

Gaudreault, André, and Philippe Marion. 2004. Transécriture and narrative mediatics: The stakes of intermediality. In *A Companion to Literature and Film*, ed. Robert Stam and Alessandra Raengo, trans. Robert Stam, 58–70. Malden, MA: Blackwell.

Genette, Gérard. 1980 [1972]. *Narrative Discourse: An Essay in Method*. Translated by Jane E. Lewin. Ithaca, NY: Cornell University Press.

Giannoukakis, Marinos. 2016. Narrative in form: A topological study of meaning in transmedial narratives. *Organised Sound* 21: 260–272.

Godoy, Hélio. 2007. Documentary realism, sampling theory and Peircean semiotics: Electronic audiovisual signs (analog or digital) as indexes of reality. *Doc On-line* 2: 107–117.

Goodman, Nelson. 1981. Twisted tales; or story, study, and symphony. In *On Narrative*, ed. W.J.T. Mitchell, 99–115. Chicago and London: The University of Chicago Press.

Gorbman, Claudia. 1987. *Unheard Melodies: Narrative Film Music.* Bloomington: Indiana University Press.

Grabócz, Márta. 2008. Classical narratology and narrative analysis in music. In *A Sounding of Signs: Modalities and Moments in Music, Culture, and Philosophy*, ed. Robert S. Hatten, Pirjo Kukkonen, Richard Littlefield, Harri Veivo, and Irma Vierimaa, 19–42. Imatra: International Semiotics Institute.

Grishakova, Marina. 2008. Literariness, fictionality, and the theory of possible worlds. In *Narrativity, Fictionality, and Literariness: The Narrative Turn and the Study of Literary Fiction*, ed. Lars-Åke Skalin, 57–76. Örebro: Örebro University Press.

Grishakova, Marina, and Marie-Laure Ryan, eds. 2010. *Intermediality and Storytelling.* Berlin and New York: De Gruyter.

Groensteen, Thierry. 2013 [2011]. *Comics and Narration.* Translated by Ann Miller. Jackson: University Press of Mississippi.

Harshaw, Benjamin. 1984. Fictionality and fields of reference: Remarks on a theoretical framework. *Poetics Today* 5: 227–251.

Hatten, Robert. 1991. On narrativity in music: Expressive genres and levels of discourse in Beethoven. *Indiana Theory Review* 12: 75–98.

Hausken, Liv. 2004. Textual theory and blind spots in media studies. In *Narrative across Media: The Languages of Storytelling*, ed. Marie-Laure Ryan, 391–403. Lincoln and London: University of Nebraska Press.

Hayles, N. Katherine. 2001. The transformation of narrative and the materiality of hypertext. *Narrative* 9: 21–39.

Heider, Fritz, and Marianne Simmel. 1944. An experimental study of apparent behavior. *The American Journal of Psychology* 57: 243–259.

Hensher, Jonathan. 2016. Glimpsing the devil's tale? Towards a visual narratology of the fantastic in illustrated editions of Cazotte's *Le Diable amoureux. Journal for Eighteenth-Century Studies* 39: 663–681.

Herman, David. 2002. *Story Logic: Problems and Possibilities of Narrative.* Lincoln and London: University of Nebraska Press.

———. 2004. Toward a transmedial narratology. In *Narrative across Media: The Languages of Storytelling*, ed. Marie-Laure Ryan, 47–75. Lincoln and London: University of Nebraska Press.

Herrnstein Smith, Barbara. 1981. Narrative versions, narrative theories. In *On Narrative*, ed. W.J.T. Mitchell, 209–232. Chicago and London: The University of Chicago Press.

Hirsch, Marianne. 1997. *Family Frames: Photography, Narrative, and Postmemory.* Cambridge, MA: Harvard University Press.

Hoffmann, Christian R., ed. 2010. *Narrative Revisited: Telling a Story in the Age of New Media.* Amsterdam and Philadelphia: John Benjamins.

Holland, Norman N. 2002. Where is a text? A neurological view. *New Literary History* 33: 21–38.

Hünig, Wolfgang K. 1974. *Strukturen des Comic strip: Ansätze zu einer textlinguistisch-semiotischen Analyse narrativer comics.* Hildesheim: Olms.

Jenkins, Henry. 2008. *Convergence Culture: Where Old and New Media Collide.* Updated and with a new afterword. New York and London: New York University Press.

Johnson, Mark. 1987. *The Body in the Mind: The Bodily Basis of Meaning, Imagination, and Reason.* Chicago and London: University of Chicago Press.

Jost, François. 2004. The look. From film to novel: An essay in comparative narratology. In *A Companion to Literature and Film*, ed. Robert Stam and Alessandra Raengo, trans. Robert Stam, 71–80. Malden, MA: Blackwell.

Kafalenos, Emma. 1996. Implications of narrative in painting and photography. *New Novel Review* 3: 53–64.

Kibédi Varga, A. 1988. Stories told by pictures. *Style* 22: 194–208.

Köhler, Wolfgang. 1929. *Gestalt Psychology.* New York: Horace Liveright.

Kramer, Lawrence. 1991. Musical narratology. *Indiana Theory Review* 12: 141–162.

Kress, Gunther, and Theo van Leeuwen. 1996. *Reading Images: The Grammar of Visual Design.* London and New York: Routledge.

Kukkonen, Karin. 2011. Comics as a test case for transmedial narratology. *SubStance* 40: 34–52.

Kutschke, Beate. 2015. Semiotische Grundlegung musikalischer Narration. In *Musik und Narration: Philosophische und musikästhetische Perspektiven*, ed. Frédéric Döhl and Daniel Martin Feige, 193–225. Bielefeld: Transcript.

Labov, William. 1972. *Language in the Inner City: Studies in the Black English Vernacular.* Philadelphia: University of Pennsylvania Press.

Lavin, Marilyn Aronberg. 1990. *The Place of Narrative: Mural Decoration in Italian Churches, 431–1600.* Chicago: University of Chicago Press.

Liu, Annie Yen-Ling. 2015. Text, topics, and formal language: Musical narrativity in Franz Liszt's *Prometheus* and *Tasso*. *Language and Semiotic Studies* 1: 139–160.

Lutas, Liviu. 2016. Storyworlds and paradoxical narration: Putting classification to a transmedial test. In *Narrative Theory, Literature and New Media: Narrative Minds and Virtual Worlds*, ed. Mari Hatavara, Matti Hyvärinen, Maria Mäkelä, and Frans Mäyrä, 29–49. London and New York: Routledge.

Mahne, Nicole. 2007. *Transmediale Erzähltheorie: Eine Einführung.* Göttingen: Vandenhoeck & Ruprecht.

Mandler, Jean M. 1992. How to build a baby: II. Conceptual primitives. *Psychological Review* 99: 587–604.

Marshall, Sandra K., and Annabel J. Cohen. 1988. Effects of musical soundtracks on attitudes toward animated geometric figures. *Music Perception* 6: 95–112.

Maus, Fred Everett. 1991. Music as narrative. *Indiana Theory Review* 12: 1–34.
McClary, Susan. 1994. Narratives of bourgeois subjectivity in Mozart's *Prague Symphonie*. In *Understanding Narrative*, ed. James Phelan and Peter J. Rabinowitz, 65–98. Columbus: Ohio State University Press.
———. 1997. The impromptu that trod on a loaf: Or how music tells stories. *Narrative* 5: 20–35.
McClatchie, Stephen. 1997. Narrative theory and music: Or, the tale of Kundry's tale. *Canadian University Music Review* 18 (1): 18.
Meelberg, Vincent. 2006. *New Sounds, New Stories: Narrativity in Contemporary Music*. Leiden: Leiden University Press.
Micznik, Vera. 2001. Music and narrative revisited: Degrees of narrativity in Beethoven and Mahler. *Journal of the Royal Musical Association* 126: 193–249.
Mikkonen, Kai. 2011. Graphic narratives as a challenge to transmedial narratology: The question of focalization. *Amerikastudien/American Studies* 56: 637–652.
Mildorf, Jarmila, and Till Kinzel. 2016a. Audionarratology: Prolegomena to a research paradigm exploring sound and narrative. In *Audionarratology: Interfaces of Sound and Narrative*, ed. Jarmila Mildorf and Till Kinzel, 1–26. Berlin and Boston: De Gruyter.
———. 2016b. *Audionarratology: Interfaces of Sound and Narrative*. Berlin and Boston: De Gruyter.
Mittell, Jason. 2014. Strategies of storytelling on transmedia television. In *Storyworlds across Media: Toward a Media-Conscious Narratology*, ed. Marie-Laure Ryan and Jan-Noël Thon, 253–277. Lincoln and London: University of Nebraska Press.
Nanay, Bence. 2009. Narrative pictures. *Journal of Aesthetics & Art Criticism* 67: 119–129.
Nash, Cristopher, ed. 1990. *Narrative in Culture: The Uses of Storytelling in the Sciences, Philosophy, and Literature*. London and New York: Routledge.
Neitzel, Britta. 2005. Levels of play and narration. In *Narratology beyond Literary Criticism: Mediality, Disciplinarity*, ed. Jan Christoph Meister, Tom Kindt, and Wilhelm Schernus, 45–64. Berlin and New York: Walter De Gruyter.
Neubauer, John. 1997. Tales of Hoffmann and others: On narrativizations of instrumental music. In *Interart Poetics: Essays on the Interrelations of the Arts and Media*, ed. Ulla-Britta Lagerroth, Hans Lund, and Erik Hedling, 117–136. Amsterdam and Atlanta, GA: Rodopi.
Newcomb, Anthony. 1987. Schumann and late eighteenth-century narrative strategies. *19th-Century Music* 11: 164–174.
Nünning, Vera, ed. 2015. *Unreliable Narration and Trustworthiness: Intermedial and Interdisciplinary Perspectives*. Berlin: De Gruyter.
Nünning, Vera, and Ansgar Nünning, eds. 2002. *Erzähltheorie transgenerisch, intermedial, interdisziplinär*. Trier: WVT Wissenshaftlicher Verlag Trier.

Page, Ruth, ed. 2010. *New Perspectives on Narrative and Multimodality*. London and New York: Routledge.
Pavel, Thomas G. 1986. *Fictional Worlds*. Cambridge, MA: Harvard University Press.
Pawlowska, Malgorzata. 2014. Musical narratology: An outline. In *Beyond Classical Narration: Transmedial and Unnatural Challenges*, ed. Jan Alber and Per Krogh Hansen, 197–220. Berlin and Boston: De Gruyter.
Peirce, Charles Sanders. 1932. *The Collected Papers of Charles Sanders Peirce [CP], Vol. 2*, ed. Charles Hartshorne and Paul Weiss. Cambridge, MA: Harvard University Press.
———. 1958. *The Collected Papers of Charles Sanders Peirce [CP], Vol. 8*, ed. Arthur W. Burks. Cambridge, MA: Harvard University Press.
Prince, Gerald. 1982. *Narratology: The Form and Functioning of Narrative*. Berlin: Mouton.
Psarra, Sophia. 2009. *Architecture and Narrative: The Formation of Space and Cultural Meaning*. London and New York: Routledge.
Ramachandran, Vilayanur S., and William Hirstein. 1997. Three laws of qualia: What neurology tells us about the biological functions of consciousness. *Journal of Consciousness Studies* 4: 429–457.
Ranta, Michael. 2013. (Re-)creating order: Narrativity and implied world views in pictures. *Storyworlds* 5: 1–30.
Ribière, Mireille, and Jan Baetens, eds. 2001. *Time, Narrative & the Fixed Image/ Temps, Narration & Image Fixe*. Amsterdam and Atlanta, GA: Rodopi.
Richardson, Brian. 1988. Point of view in drama: Diegetic monologue, unreliable narrators, and the author's voice on stage. *Comparative Drama* 22: 193–214.
Rimmon-Kenan, Shlomith. 1989. How the model neglects the medium: Linguistics, language, and the crisis of narratology. *Journal of Narrative Technique* 19: 157–166.
Ronen, Ruth. 1988. Completing the incompleteness of fictional entities. *Poetics Today* 9: 497–514.
Ryan, Marie-Laure. 1980. Fiction, non-factuals, and the principle of minimal departure. *Poetics* 9: 403–422.
———. 1984. Fiction as a logical, ontological, and illocutionary issue. *Style* 18: 121–139.
———. 1991. *Possible Worlds, Artificial Intelligence, and Narrative Theory*. Bloomington and Indianapolis: Indiana University Press.
———. 2004a. Introduction. In *Narrative across Media: The Languages of Storytelling*, ed. Marie-Laure Ryan, 1–40. Lincoln and London: University of Nebraska Press.
———, ed. 2004b. *Narrative across Media: The Languages of Storytelling*. Lincoln and London: University of Nebraska Press.

———. 2005. On the theoretical foundations of transmedial narratology. In *Narratology Beyond Literary Criticism: Mediality, Disciplinarity*, ed. Jan Christoph Meister, Tom Kindt, and Wilhelm Schernus, 1–23. Berlin and New York: Walter De Gruyter.

———. 2006. *Avatars of Story*. Minneapolis and London: University of Minnesota Press.

———. 2007. Diagramming narrative. *Semiotica* 165: 11–40.

———. 2013. Transmedial storytelling and transfictionality. *Poetics Today* 34: 361–388.

Ryan, Marie-Laure, and Jan-Noël Thon, eds. 2014. *Storyworlds across Media: Toward a Media-Conscious Narratology*. Lincoln and London: University of Nebraska Press.

Scholes, Robert. 1981. Language, narrative, and anti-narrative. In *On Narrative*, ed. W.J.T. Mitchell, 200–208. Chicago and London: The University of Chicago Press.

Schnackertz, Hermann Josef. 1980. *Form und Funktion medialen Erzählens: Narrativität in Bildsequenz und Comicstrip*. Munich: Wilhelm Fink.

Schwanecke, Christine. 2012. *Intermedial Storytelling: Thematisation, Imitation and Incorporation of Photography in English and American Fiction at the Turn of the 21st Century*. Trier: Wissenschaftlicher Verlag Trier.

Searle, John R. 1975. The logical status of fictional discourse. *New Literary History* 6: 319–332.

Seaton, Douglass. 2005. Narrative in music: The case of Beethoven's 'Tempest' sonata. In *Narratology Beyond Literary Criticism: Mediality, Disciplinarity*, ed. Jan Christoph Meister, Tom Kindt, and Wilhelm Schernus, 65–81. Berlin and New York: Walter De Gruyter.

Skov Nielsen, Henrik, James Phelan, and Richard Walsh. 2015. Ten theses about fictionality. *Narrative* 23: 61–73.

Smith, Murray. 2009. Double trouble: On film, fiction, and narrative. *Storyworlds* 1: 1–23.

Smuts, Aaron. 2009. Story identity and story type. *Journal of Aesthetics & Art Criticism* 67: 5–13.

Steiner, Wendy. 1988. *Pictures of Romance: Form against Context in Painting and Literature*. Chicago: Chicago University Press.

Stern, Barbara B. 1994. Classical and vignette television advertising dramas: Structural models, formal analysis, and consumer effects. *Journal of Consumer Research* 20: 601–615.

Tarasti, Eero. 1994. *A Theory of Musical Semiotics*. Bloomington: Indiana University Press.

Thibault, Mattia. 2016. Notes on the narratological approach to board games. *KOME: An International Journal of Pure Communication Inquiry* 4: 74–81.

Thompson, Kristin. 2003. *Storytelling in Film and Television*. Cambridge, MA: Harvard University Press.

Thon, Jan-Noël. 2015. Narratives across media and the outlines of a media-conscious narratology. In *Handbook of Intermediality: Literature—Image—Sound—Music*, ed. Gabriele Rippl, 439–456. Berlin and Boston: De Gruyter.

———. 2016. *Transmedial Narratology and Contemporary Media Culture*. Lincoln and London: University of Nebraska Press.

Tomashevsky, Boris. 2012 [1925]. Thematics. In *Russian Formalist Criticism: Four Essays*, ed. Lee T. Lemon and Marion J. Reis, trans. Lee T. Lemon and Marion J. Reis, 2nd ed., 61–95. Lincoln and London: University of Nebraska Press.

Walsh, Richard. 2007. *The Rhetoric of Fictionality: Narrative Theory and the Idea of Fiction*. Columbus: The Ohio State University Press.

Walton, Kendall L. 1983. Fiction, fiction-making, and styles of fictionality. *Philosophy and Literature* 7: 78–88.

Weitzmann, Kurt. 1947. *Illustrations in Roll and Codex: A Study of the Origin and Method of Text Illustration*. Princeton, NJ: Princeton University Press.

White, Hayden. 1981. The value of narrativity in the representation of reality. In *On Narrative*, ed. W.J.T. Mitchell, 1–23. Chicago and London: The University of Chicago Press.

Wickhoff, Franz. 1895. Der Stil der Genesisbilder und die Geschichte seiner Entwicklung. In *Die Wiener Genesis*, ed. Wilhelm Ritter von Härtel and Franz Wickhoff, vol. 2, 1–96. Vienna: F. Tempsky.

Wildekamp, Ada, Ineke van Montfoort, and Willem van Ruiswijk. 1980. Fictionality and convention. *Poetics* 9: 547–567.

Wolf, Werner. 2003. Narrative and narrativity: A narratological reconceptualization and its applicability to the visual arts. *Word & Image* 19: 180–197.

———. 2004. 'Cross the border—Close that gap': Towards an intermedial narratology. *European Journal of English Studies* 8: 81–103.

———. 2011. Narratology and media(lity): The transmedial expansion of a literary discipline and possible consequences. In *Current Trends in Narratology*, ed. Greta Olson, 145–180. Berlin and New York: De Gruyter.

———. 2014. Framings of narrative in literature and the pictorial arts. In *Storyworlds across Media: Toward a Media-Conscious Narratology*, ed. Marie-Laure Ryan and Jan-Noël Thon, 126–147. Lincoln and London: University of Nebraska Press.

———. 2017. Transmedial narratology: Theoretical foundations and some applications (fiction, single pictures, instrumental music). *Narrative* 25: 256–285.

Yadav, Alok. 2010. Literature, fictiveness, and postcolonial criticism. *Novel* 43: 189–196.

INDEX

A
Abbate, Carolyn, 8
Abbott, Lawrence L., 8
Actions, *see* Events
Actual world, *see* Perceived actual sphere
Alber, Jan, 69
Almén, Byron, 8
Alpers, Svetlana, 8
Altman, Rick, 7
Aristotle, 107
Arvidson, Mats, 9
Aural, *see* Hearing, sense of

B
Background knowledge, *see* Collateral experience
Baetens, Jan, 8
Bal, Mieke, 38
Barthes, Roland, 7, 57, 83
Basic media, *see* Media types
Bassili, John N., 99, 100
Bergman, Mats, 25, 28
Berning, Nora, 9
Booth, Wayne C., 68, 70
Bordwell, David, 7, 8, 40
Branigan, Edward, 40, 97
Bremond, Claude, 7
Brewer, William F., 26
Brilliant, Richard, 8
Brooks, Peter, 8
Bundgaard, Peer F., 41, 100

C
Campbell, Richard, 8
Canary, Robert H., 8
Chatman, Seymour, 7, 8, 38, 46, 78–79, 99
Cognitive import, 22–30, 37, 48–51, 64, 65, 104–105
Cognitive schemata, 40–41, 47, 89, 99, 123, 130
Cohen, Annabel J., 100
Coherence, *see* Internal coherence
Cohn, Dorrit, 8
Colapietro, Vincent, 107
Collateral experience, 25–26, 30–32, 39–41, 45, 72, 89, 98–100, 105, 118, 123, 127
Communication (definition), 21, 22

Contiguity (ground of indices), 27, 29, 50, 56, 79, 96–101, 104–111, 119, 124, 127, 128, 132–133
Convention, *see* Habit (ground of symbols)

D
D'Alessandro, William, 109
de Freitas, Elizabeth, 8
de Saussure, Ferdinand, 11
Diehl, Nicholas, 69
Discourse, 11, 13, 38, 123
Doxiadis, Apostolos, 8
Duration, *see* Events

E
Eakin, John Paul, 8
Earlier communication, *see* Other virtual spheres
Einstein, Albert, 126
Events
  actions, 80–83, 96–97, 104, 117, 122, 126, 130–131
  duration of events, 92, 123, 128, 131
  frequency of events, 92, 118, 123, 124, 128, 131
  hierarchies of events, 82–83, 117, 123, 126, 130
  occurrences, 80–83, 97, 117, 122–123, 126, 130–131
  order of events, 54–56, 87, 91–92, 118–119, 121, 123–129, 131
Existents, 78–82, 85, 101, 117, 121–123, 126
External truthfulness, 57, 61, 98, 103–111, 133
Extracommunicational domain, 26–30, 38–41, 64, 66–71, 98, 104–108

F
Fiction, 106–111, 119
Fictionality, 61, 104, 107–109, 124
  See also External truthfulness
Fludernik, Monika, 8, 40, 99
Focalization, 72–74, 123, 128, 132
Foster, Susan Leigh, 8
Framing, 98–100
Frequency, *see* Events

G
Gale, Richard M., 107, 109
Gallagher, Catherine, 107
Gaudreault, André, 8, 39, 69
Genette, Gérard, 38, 72, 73, 83, 92, 118, 123, 131
Gestalt, 28–30, 45, 68, 95, 98, 107–109
Gewirtz, Paul, 8
Giannoukakis, Marinos, 9
Godoy, Hélio, 98
Goodman, Nelson, 8
Gorbman, Claudia, 8
Grabócz, Márta, 119
Grishakova, Marina, 9, 109
Groensteen, Thierry, 40

H
Habit (ground of symbols), 50, 55–57, 88–93, 113, 117–119, 121–122, 127
Harshaw, Benjamin, 109
Hatten, Robert, 123
Hausken, Liv, 10–12
Hayles, N. Katherine, 8
Hearing, sense of, 3–4, 9, 23, 25, 47–52, 56–58, 67, 71–72, 79, 87, 88, 92, 100–101, 120–124, 130
Heider, Fritz, 99–100
Hensher, Jonathan, 72

Herman, David, 40, 47, 78
Herrnstein Smith, Barbara, 13
Hierarchies, *see* Events
Hirsch, Marianne, 8
Hirstein, William, 31
Hoffmann, Christian R., 9
Holland, Norman N., 31
Hünig, Wolfgang K., 8

I
Icons, *see* Sign types
Images, 3, 4, 8–9, 47, 51–58, 70–72, 78–79, 88, 101, 107, 116–118, 129
  See also Icons; Sign types
Image scheme, 30–32, 78
Implied author, 68
Implied reader, 70
Indices, *see* Sign types
Intermediality, 5, 9, 11, 48
Internal coherence, 29–32, 57, 61, 68, 95–101, 103, 123, 127, 128, 131
Interoception, 26, 65
Interpretant, *see* Sign constituents
Intracommunicational domain, 26–29, 38, 64, 68, 71, 96–99, 101, 105, 108
Introspection, 26, 65

J
Jenkins, Henry, 6
Johnson, Mark, 31, 40
Jost, François, 72

K
Kafalenos, Emma, 8, 40, 117
Kibédi Varga, A., 118
Kinzel, Till, 9, 73
Köhler, Wolfgang, 30
Kozicki, Henry, 8

Kramer, Lawrence, 8
Kress, Gunther, 8
Kukkonen, Karin, 57
Kutschke, Beate, 9

L
Labov, William, 8, 36
Language, *see* Verbal media
Lavin, Marilyn Aronberg, 8
Liu, Annie Yen-Ling, 9
Lutas, Liviu, 10

M
Mahne, Nicole, 8
Mandler, Jean M., 31, 40
Marion, Philippe, 8, 39
Marshall, Sandra K., 100
Materiality, 5, 13, 22–24, 28, 41, 48–54, 58, 78–80, 86, 96–98, 100, 101, 107–111, 116, 119–120, 124, 125, 128, 129, 132–133
Maus, Fred Everett, 123, 124
McClary, Susan, 122
McClatchie, Stephen, 8
Meaning, *see* Cognitive import
Meaningful interrelations, *see* Internal coherence
Media characteristics (definition), 5
Media modalities, 45–58, 61, 68–71, 86, 100–101, 113, 125, 129
Media modes, *see* Media modalities
Media product (definition), 22
Media traits, *see* Media characteristics (definition); Media modalities
Media types
  basic media types, 51–53, 56, 57, 69, 86, 100, 107, 111, 116, 133
  qualified media types, 51–53, 108, 115–133
Mediation, 22–24, 48–49, 67

Medium-specificity, 4, 9–15, 36, 47, 71, 73, 116, 133
Meelberg, Vincent, 36–41
Meister, Jan Christoph, 81
Micznik, Vera, 122
Mikkonen, Kai, 72
Mildorf, Jarmila, 9, 73
Mittell, Jason, 6
Multimodality, 9, 57–58, 100–101, 107, 125, 129–131

N
Nanay, Bence, 78
Narratee
  actual narratee, 65–68, 87, 100, 129–132
  virtual narratee, 66, 70, 71
Narration (definition), 37
Narrative (definition), 36, 37
Narrativization, 98–100, 117, 130
Narrator
  actual narrator, 66, 67, 90–92, 129–132
  virtual narrator, 66, 69, 71, 77, 123, 128, 130–132
Nash, Cristopher, 8
Neitzel, Britta, 8
Neubauer, John, 100
Newcomb, Anthony, 8, 121–122
Nonfiction, *see* Fiction
Nünning, Ansgar, 9
Nünning, Vera, 9

O
Object, *see* Sign constituents
Occurrences, *see* Events
Order, *see* Events
Other virtual spheres, 64, 67, 104–111, 133
  See also Extracommunicational domain

P
Page, Ruth, 9
Pavel, Thomas G., 107
Pawlowska, Malgorzata, 119
Peirce, Charles Sanders, 11, 23–24, 39–41, 49–50, 58
Perceived actual sphere, 64–67, 98, 104–111, 119, 124, 128, 129, 132–133
  See also Extracommunicational domain
Prince, Gerald, 36, 70
Proprioception, 26, 65
Psarra, Sophia, 8

Q
Qualified media, *see* Media types

R
Ramachandran, Vilayanur S., 31
Ranta, Michael, 40, 47
Real connection, *see* Contiguity (ground of indices)
Reeves, Jimmie L., 8
Representamen, *see* Sign constituents
Representation (definition), 22–24
Represented events, *see* Events
Resemblance, *see* Similarity (ground of icons)
Ribière, Mireille, 8
Richardson, Brian, 8
Rimmon-Kenan, Shlomith, 7–8
Ronen, Ruth, 109
Ryan, Marie-Laure, 6–9, 26–27, 30, 40, 41, 46, 57, 109

S
Schnackertz, Hermann Josef, 8
Scholes, Robert, 58
Schwanecke, Christine, 9

Searle, John R., 107–110
Seaton, Douglas, 122
Semiotics, 11, 40, 57, 58
　presemiotic modalities, 23, 48–51,
　　53–54, 57, 58, 120, 121
　semiotic modality, 49–53,
　　56–58, 86, 100–101, 120,
　　121, 129
Sensoriality, 22–25, 30–32, 39, 48–58,
　69, 71–74, 80, 86–87, 91–92,
　98–101, 116, 129
Sequential decoding, 55, 88, 118,
　127
Sight, sense of, 3, 8–9, 25, 30, 31,
　47–58, 68–73, 79, 82, 87, 88,
　91, 92, 98, 100–101, 105, 110,
　115–121, 125, 129
Sign constituents, 24
　interpretant, 23–28, 39, 64, 80
　object, 23–30, 38–40, 49–51,
　　54–57, 68, 79, 86, 88, 89,
　　96–98, 101, 103–111, 116,
　　119, 124, 128, 133
　representamen, 23–25, 49–51,
　　54–57, 79, 86, 96, 101, 104,
　　133
Sign types, 49–50, 54, 58
　icons, 23, 49–52, 56–58, 69–72,
　　79, 82, 87–89, 92, 100–101,
　　116–122, 125
　indices, 27, 29, 49–50, 56–58, 79,
　　88, 96–98, 100–101, 109,
　　119, 122, 124, 127–129,
　　132–133
　symbols, 47–50, 52, 55–58, 79, 82,
　　88, 99–101, 117–127
Similarity (ground of icons), 49–50,
　57, 79, 116, 120, 125
Simmel, Marianne, 99–100
Skov Nielsen, Henrik, 108
Smell, sense of, 49, 56
Smith, Murray, 36

Smuts, Aaron, 37
Spatiotemporality, 5, 14, 23, 25,
　30–32, 36–41, 46, 48–56, 58, 61,
　66–67, 72, 74, 78–80, 83, 85–93,
　95–97, 99–101, 105, 116,
　118–129, 131–132
States, 79–82, 85, 90–93, 117, 123,
　126–133
Steiner, Wendy, 8
Stern, Barbara B., 8
Story (definition), 37
Storyworld, 12, 30, 73
Symbols, *see* Sign types

T
Tarasti, Eero, 121, 122
Taste, sense of, 56, 57, 72
Texts, *see* Verbal media
Thibault, Mattia, 9
Thompson, Kristin, 8
Thon, Jan-Noël, 9, 12–13, 30, 38, 63,
　72
Tomashevsky, Boris, 82–83, 92
Touch, sense of, 25, 49, 56–57, 71,
　88, 116
Transmedia storytelling, 6
Transmediality, 5–6, 10, 37, 54, 74,
　78–79
Transmediation, 5–6, 9–10, 14, 79,
　83, 116, 125–127, 133
Truth, 103, 104, 110, 111
Truthfulness, *see* External
　truthfulness

V
van Leeuwen, Theo, 8
Verbal media, 4, 7–10, 36, 40, 47–48,
　52–58, 66, 69, 71, 79, 88,
　117–119, 125–127, 129
　See also Sign types; Symbols

Virtual sphere, 27–32, 46, 55–57, 77–83, 87–92, 95–101, 103–111, 122–123, 125–129, 133
  See also Intracommunicational domain
Vision, *see* Sight, sense of

W
Walsh, Richard, 7
Walton, Kendall L., 107

Weitzmann, Kurt, 118
White, Hayden, 8
Wickhoff, Franz, 118
Wildekamp, Ada, 111
Wolf, Werner, 8, 46–48, 99, 117–119
Woolf, Virginia, 28

Y
Yadav, Alok, 109

The manufacturer's authorised representative in the EU is Springer Nature Customer Service Centre GmbH, Europaplatz 3, 69115 Heidelberg, Germany. If you have any concerns regarding our products, please contact ProductSafety@springernature.com

Printed and bound by CPI Group (UK) Ltd, Croydon, CR0 4YY
23/03/2026
02076447-0011